# TRAINING AND SUPERVISION FOR COUNSELLING

## IN

*Action*

**COUNSELLING**
**· IN ACTION ·**

---

Series editor: Windy Dryden

Counselling in Action is a series of books developed especially for counsellors and students of counselling which provides clear and explicit guidelines for counselling practice.
A special feature of the series is the emphasis it places on the process of counselling.

# TRAINING AND
# SUPERVISION FOR
# COUNSELLING
## IN Action

Edited by
**WINDY DRYDEN**
**AND BRIAN THORNE**

**SAGE Publications**
London • Newbury Park • New Delhi

First published 1991

SAGE Publications Ltd
6 Bonhill Street
London EC2A 4PU

SAGE Publications Inc
2455 Teller Road
Newbury Park, California 91320

SAGE Publications India Pvt Ltd
32, M-Block Market
Greater Kailash – I
New Delhi 110 048

**British Library Cataloguing in Publication data**

Training and supervision for counselling in action.
– (Counselling in action)
   I. Dryden, Windy    Thorne, Brian    III. Series
   361.307

   ISBN 0–8039–8335–2
   ISBN 0–8039–8336–0 pbk

**Library of Congress catalog card number 91-052785**

Typeset by Photoprint, Torquay
Printed in Great Britain by Dotesios Ltd, Trowbridge, Wiltshire

# Contents

# Dedication

We would like to dedicate this book to the officers and members of the British Association for Counselling.

# Acknowledgements

We would like to thank the following people who gave freely of their time in helping us prepare Chapter 2: Mary Charleton, representing the South West London Counselling Course now based at Southwark College; and Ellen Noonan and Paul Terry, representing the counselling courses at the Extra-Mural Centre of the University of London at Birkbeck College.

# Preface

The purpose of this book in the Counselling in Action series is to explore in some depth the issues involved in the training and supervision of counsellors and in the preparation of those who are to undertake supervisory and training roles. The book also provides examples of good practice drawn from different counselling traditions. It is hoped that it will prove to be an invaluable resource for those engaged in supervision and training and will also serve as a reliable guide to those who are seeking to establish new courses in the years ahead.

We believe that such a book is particularly appropriate at this point in the historical development of counselling in Britain. Counselling is now a well-established activity and its usefulness has been demonstrated in many different domains. The British Association for Counselling currently has more than 6,000 individual members and a large number of organizations and agencies in corporate membership. Furthermore it has now produced its own schemes for the accreditation not only of individual practitioners but also for the recognition of training courses and supervisors. Similar steps are being taken towards a process for recognizing trainers. It is clear that these important initiatives by the Association will engender an increasing concern both within the counselling movement and among potential clients for the establishment of the highest possible standards in the supervision and training of counsellors.

There is always a danger that a concern for high standards can result in a rigidity of practice and a stultifying of imaginative innovations. The book provides an important antidote to such a development by drawing both on the experience of trainers and supervisors (many of whom have been notable and intrepid pioneers during the past decade) and that of trainees and supervisees.

Windy Dryden, London
Brian Thorne, Norwich

# Abbreviations

| | |
|---|---|
| BAC | British Association for Counselling |
| CDT | community designed time |
| FDI | Facilitator Development Institute (Britain) |
| ILEA | Inner London Education Authority |
| NLP | Neuro-linguistic Programming |
| PDG | personal development group |
| SWLC | South West London College |
| TA | Transactional Analysis |
| WPF | Westminster Pastoral Foundation |

# Contributors

*Rose Battye*   Counsellor in General Practice, Norwich
*Petrūska Clarkson*   metanoia Psychotherapy Training Institute, London
*Windy Dryden*   Goldsmiths' College, London
*Maria Gilbert*   metanoia Psychotherapy Training Institute, London
*Peter Hawkins*   Director, Bath Counselling and Psychotherapy Courses, and Consultant, Bath Associates
*Dave Mearns*   Jordanhill College of Education, Glasgow and PCT (Britain)
*Judy Moore*   University of East Anglia, Norwich
*Brigid Proctor*   Private Practice, London
*Campbell Purton*   University of East Anglia and Ber Street Centre, Norwich
*Robin Shohet*   Private Practice, London and Malvern
*Brian Thorne*   University of East Anglia and The Norwich Centre, Norwich
*Joan Wilmot*   Private Practice, London and Malvern

# PART 1  TRAINING

## 1  Key Issues in the Training of Counsellors

### Brian Thorne and Windy Dryden

**Counselling comes of age**

When at the beginning of 1985 the British Association for Counselling set up its Working Group on the Recognition of Counsellor Training Courses it could justifiably be said that counselling had come of age in Britain. Interestingly enough this event occurred almost 20 years after the first appearance of full-time British counsellor training programmes (in the universities of Reading and Keele) and some five years after the Association's initial scheme for the accreditation of individual counsellors. Only after such a lengthy gestation period, it seemed, was the counselling movement sufficiently confident of its own coherence and identity to begin in earnest on the detailed study of what it is that is required to equip a person to fulfil the arduous and demanding role of the professional counsellor. Indeed, it is only comparatively recently that the notion of a counselling profession as such has gained widespread acceptance and in some circles the image of the counsellor as a well-meaning but essentially untrained dispenser of comfort and sympathy continues to die hard.

Inevitably, the early training programmes were, to a large extent, in the hands of non-counsellors and as a result the focus of training was often uncertain. Clinical and educational psychologists, social workers and psychiatrists, and even psychoanalysts, were involved in the formation of an essentially new kind of therapeutic helper, and not unnaturally they tended to develop models of training which were much coloured by their own experience and professional identities. Furthermore there was a sense in which trainees were made to feel that they were being prepared for an activity which was essentially ancillary to or even inferior to the more 'professional' work of their trainers. The saving grace in all this was undoubtedly the frequent presence of American practitioners on the staff of those courses which developed in British universities during the late 1960s and 1970s. Distinguished professors of counselling, eminent both in practice and scholarship, were keen to take up Fulbright awards in the United Kingdom, and as a result leading figures in the American counsellor-education field made substantial contributions in these early years to the work of counsellor training courses in the Universities of Keele, Reading and Aston in Birmingham. Many of the students from these pioneering courses subsequently gained posts of influence, particularly in educational institutions, and it was not long before many of them found themselves taking a training role in addition to their clinical work. The emergence of the British practitioner/ trainer had a significant effect on training provision for it was now increasingly possible to design courses which drew on the actual experience of practising British counsellors as well as on the well-established tradition from across the Atlantic. Gradually, too, trainers from other disciplines lost their primary role and courses became more clearly focused as they passed into the hands of those who were proud to call themselves counsellors and did not owe their principal allegiance to another profession.

Not all the developments prior to 1985 took place on the campuses of universities and polytechnics. The Marriage Guidance Council (MGC) in particular was much preoccupied with its training procedures and it is not without significance that the very word 'counsellor' was for many years associated mainly with MGC and its work in the field of marital and relationship difficulties. The increasing demand for the services of marriage-guidance counsellors presented the Council with formidable challenges in the training field and it is no small tribute to the dedication and imagination of marriage-guidance trainers that 'Relate', as it is now called, is currently responding to more clients than ever and that both the numbers and the effectiveness of counsellors operating in this context have increased out of all recognition.

The field of pastoral care and counselling was perhaps the other most influential area for training initiatives. Here, again, many of the pioneers drew extensively on American experience, but the long tradition of social involvement in the British churches meant that there were many Christians, both ordained and lay, who were keen to apply the insights of counselling psychology to the care of hurt and wounded souls in their own communities. Frank Lake and his Clinical Theology Association and the growth of the Westminster Pastoral Foundation and its affiliated centres are two of the most striking examples of organizations where commitment to training was and remains central to their operation. Indeed, there are many people in Britain who owe much if not all of their counselling training to pastoral agencies of this kind but who would themselves claim little or no Christian allegiance. It is perhaps a mark of the strength of the pastoral care and counselling movement that it has always encouraged co-operation not only across the Christian denominations but also with the secular world of counselling and therapy. Significantly, when the British Association for Counselling was founded in 1977 it was the Association for Pastoral Care and Counselling (together with the Association for Student Counselling) which agreed to relinquish its previous independence and autonomy in order to ensure the satisfactory 'birth' of the new generic and secular organization.

The BAC Working Group on the Recognition of Counsellor Training Courses which met for the first time in January 1985 drew its membership from all the main streams of training experience and expertise described above. There were those who owed their training (and most of their clinical experience) to the universities and polytechnics while others were leading figures from the field of pastoral care and counselling. A third force was provided by a seasoned marriage-guidance tutor. What is more, many of the group had experience of training provided both by statutory educational institutions and by private agencies. Indeed, so wide and varied was the experience of the group members that it is perhaps surprising that three years later they were able to present unanimous recommendations to the British Association concerning the essential ingredients of a counsellor training programme (British Association for Counselling, 1988). In the process of their work they had been forced, sometimes painfully, to face all the key issues which the training of counsellors inevitably presents if it is to be undertaken with the seriousness and thoroughness which the counsellor's role undoubtedly requires. It is to these issues that we now turn.

**What should be learned and why**

*Self-exploration*
For the counsellor trainer one of the most daunting issues that has to be faced at the outset of any course is the fact that if things go well they will not go smoothly. The reason for this is that training, if it is to be effective, must involve a high degree of self-exploration on the part of trainees with the aim of increasing their self-awareness and self-knowledge. Even in those therapeutic traditions where the emphasis is on clients' behavioural change or the modification of cognitive processes it is nonetheless accepted that an

unaware counsellor leading an unexamined life is likely to be a liability rather than an asset. By definition, however, self-exploration leads to new discoveries and often sudden movement into unknown psychological terrain. Some of these developments are likely to be disturbing and disorienting with the result that almost all trainees at some stage of their training are likely to experience periods of distress or bewilderment and may even at times become subject to incapacitating anxiety or depression. Notoriously, too, relationships with spouses and other family members are liable to undergo considerable upheaval or even to founder altogether. The trainer is therefore presented with two closely related tasks: how to ensure that trainees are given adequate opportunity for self-exploration and how to establish the kind of structure which will hold and support those who find themselves struggling with new and unexpected discoveries about themselves.

There are those who believe that these requirements can only be met by ensuring that every trainee undergoes personal therapy as an obligatory part of training. Without such provision, it is argued, there can be no guarantee that the trainee will confront in a systematic and thorough manner those areas of his or her life and personality which are a potential source of difficulty or conflict. What is more, an insistence on personal therapy has the additional advantage of making sure that the trainee has a real and substantial experience of being in the client's chair. These are powerful arguments but not all trainers are convinced by them. Those who oppose obligatory personal therapy (and there are none, we believe, who would question the value of personal therapy which is sought voluntarily by a trainee) do so on the grounds that the therapy relationship itself can serve as a means of evading important interpersonal difficulties which may be part of the trainee's experience both within the course and in his or her personal life. Central to this criticism is the fear that some trainees will see personal therapy as *the* arena for self-exploration (within limits) and will feel entitled to remain somewhat aloof and withdrawn in other areas of the training programme. Those who espouse this point of view will place heavy emphasis on the concept of the training group itself – or a subgroup within it – as the chief therapeutic environment for the development of self-awareness. In this model the trainees are encouraged to see the course community as the context both for self-exploration and for finding support in times of particular difficulty. Trainers, supervisors and personal therapists, where they exist, may have important roles to play in offering additional or specific help but they are not there so that trainees can 'siphon off' important personal material which belongs more appropriately to the group as a whole. It should be remembered that membership of a group can itself be a powerful trigger for self-exploration. Groups and organizations frequently present individuals with new challenges and new threats which can only be faced by a willingness to be open to the strengths and vulnerabilities that are thereby revealed. In this way the course community may well serve a dual function: it can be the therapeutic arena for facing those very insights into the self which it has itself provoked.

Clearly, self-exploration can occur in a variety of different contexts and for some trainees, indeed, the opportunity to be quietly with themselves as they study for an essay or reflect on a day's work is more productive than the most dramatic encounter group. For the trainer, however, there can be no assumption that such self-exploration will take place automatically. The course design and the apportioning of time must reflect the high priority given to ensuring that such exploration is central to the counsellor's apprenticeship and not an optional extra. What is more, a course through its structure, needs to recognize that many and possibly all trainees will experience pain and distress as they gradually confront themselves more honestly and courageously: they should not be left with nowhere to go and nobody to whom they can turn when such testing times occur.

*Work with clients*
Difficult as it is to believe, there are counselling courses where trainees never meet a client. The reasoning behind such a bizarre state of affairs is that fellow trainees are deemed to constitute the clientele and to provide more than enough material for counselling practice. The inadequacy of such reasoning is not difficult to expose for it is clear that trainees on a course are unlikely to be motivated by the various and often pressing needs which bring 'normal' clients to the counsellor's door. Even in those instances where genuinely felt concerns and difficulties are experienced, the fact that the 'client' is likely to be well known to the 'counsellor' introduces a factor into the therapeutic relationship which strikingly distinguishes it from the usual case-load of the practising counsellor in the ordinary course of events. Indeed, it is not uncommon for many counsellors to refuse in principle to counsel those who are friends or even passing acquaintances.

The willingness of some course organizers to settle for this unsatisfactory method of providing clients for trainees is undoubtedly prompted by the difficulty which often arises in attempting to set up a valid counselling experience for course members. It is not always easy to persuade counselling agencies to welcome trainees, and where students themselves are left with the responsibility of arranging their own placements they may find that they carry little credibility. The issues here are complex. Clearly it is essential that trainees have clients but it is also understandable that counselling agencies or general practitioners, for example, should be hesitant about letting loose unskilled beginners on their clients or patients. Questions which have to be addressed include the point at which trainees should first be permitted to see clients. From the trainer's point of view the sooner the student has some 'real' experience, the more likely it is that he or she will be able to relate theory to practice. On the other hand it could be argued that from the client's point of view, and from that of a counselling agency, it is of considerable importance that the trainee already possess a modicum of theoretical knowledge and has had some opportunity to develop basic counselling skills. Whichever policy is adopted it is clearly crucial that close and frequent supervision is provided for the trainee and that his or her case-load is kept to two or three clients at any one time for at least the initial stages of the training programme. A policy which dictates that a trainee should have only one client at a time is more questionable for there is a danger that the single client can become of such critical significance to the trainee that there is an over-investment in securing a successful 'outcome'.

The provision of supervision is often fraught with problems. Inexperienced trainees are naturally anxious and lacking in self-confidence and may require frequent reassurance. The accessibility of the supervisor, both in person and on the telephone, is of major importance and if an agency is also providing field supervision it is less than helpful to a trainee if the styles and even the therapeutic orientation of the two supervisors concerned are widely divergent. If a course only provides group supervision it is important that the group is small enough and the sessions of sufficient duration for all members to present their work regularly and in depth.

It is often claimed by students on teacher training courses that the real learning occurs on teaching practice. Much the same could be said of the counselling practice and for this reason it is desirable that trainees have the opportunity to work with a variety of clients during this training period and to experience both short- and long-term counselling relationships. The supervision requirements for such practice are considerable and there are obvious resource implications, which will be considered later.

*The acquisition of counselling skills*
Fellow trainees may not constitute an appropriate source for clientele but they undoubtedly provide the best possible milieu for

developing counselling skills. Skills training offers trainees the opportunity to isolate and analyse specific responses to clients in a way which is scarcely possible within the context of a normal counselling relationship. Such training is often enhanced by the use of audio and video equipment which permits the trainee to carry out a detached exploration of small segments of interaction and to investigate the impact of particular verbal responses and the power of non-verbal communication. The skills which are being developed may vary from one therapeutic orientation to another but the capacity to form a therapeutic alliance with clients will be common to them all. The person-centred trainee, for example, is likely to devote much attention to increasing the repertoire of empathic responses whereas the cognitive-behavioural counsellor may be keen to practise interventions which impinge on self-defeating thinking and behavioural patterns. Both trainees, however, through the intensive practice of specific skills, will be familiarizing themselves with the essential tools of their trade but will be doing this in a context where the skills cannot be divorced from attitudes and from a consideration of the relationship which is being forged with the client. At least, this must be the hope, for the danger of skills training which is conducted in a vacuum is that the trainee can emerge at the end armed with a kit of techniques and strategies but little capacity to develop the kind of relationship where those skills can be creatively employed. Trainers of all traditions have constantly to be on their guard so that they do not encourage the emergence of clever technicians rather than sensitive counsellors.

Counselling skills training is likely to take up much of the time in the formal timetabling of a course and it presents several operational difficulties. For most trainees it is likely to be one of the most threatening of their activities and has therefore to be approached with delicacy and with a regard for individual differences. Some students, for example, take readily to role-playing or to appearing on a video whereas others must work through much anxiety before they are ready to risk themselves in these ways. Trainers have to exhibit both firmness and gentleness if all participants are eventually to benefit from the various learning situations. Much sensitivity is also demanded of trainers if they are to assist trainees to give each other honest feedback during skills sessions. In the initial stages of training it is both natural and desirable that emphasis should be laid on the positive aspects of a trainee's counselling behaviour but later on it becomes a hindrance to growth if more critical comment is always withheld out of fear of hurting the trainee or undermining his or her confidence. It is often the trainer who must first model the kind of feedback which can incorporate both positive and negative reactions without losing a deep respect and caring for the trainee whose work is being observed. Once a training group has established a climate where such feedback is both offered and welcomed there is no limit to the learning which can develop in counselling skills sessions.

*Counselling theory and academic content*
Counselling courses which first developed in university settings usually found themselves saddled with academic requirements and regulations which were scarcely conducive to effective training. Frequent written work was often required during the course together with lengthy formal examinations at the end. Courses which have developed outside traditional academic institutions have tended to err in the opposite direction and have placed almost exclusive importance on experiential and practical work. It is clear, however, that counsellors who have a poor theoretical understanding of their work are likely to lose their heads (and their hearts) when confronted by difficult clients or particularly complex dilemmas. Experiential learning which is unsupported by sound theoretical understanding is likely after a while to leave the trainee confused or incapable of describing and analysing the processes he or she is experiencing with clients. At the very least there needs to be a sufficient emphasis on reading and written work to ensure that students are able to clarify philosophical and theoretical concepts and to apply them to their practical counselling work.

As with counselling skills, trainers need to be aware that for some trainees 'academic' work arouses acute anxiety and deep feelings of inadequacy, but here again course members are likely to be able to offer each other considerable support once initial fears of insensitive criticism have been allayed. For some students it may well be that progress in their ability to conceptualize their work and to discuss it intelligently with professionals from allied fields will constitute a major arena for building self-respect and enhancing self-confidence. The need to be able to communicate across professional boundaries also dictates that time is given to studying the work of such professions as psychiatry, clinical psychology and social work. It is likely, too, that many courses will be offering a training in one specific school of counselling, but this 'majoring' in a particular tradition should not preclude a comparative study of other forms of counselling. The psychodynamic counsellor who is ignorant, for example, of the person-centred approach or of cognitive therapy is scarcely in a favourable position to enter into constructive dialogue with colleagues from those other traditions or to be able to offer effective guidance to clients who may wish to be referred elsewhere.

The question of whether initial training courses *should* offer only one approach to counselling is perhaps itself debatable, although it is doubtful whether in most cases the time factor would allow in-depth training in the practice of more than one orientation. This, however, is a separate question from the comparative study of counselling theories and methodologies. In a field where it is increasingly evident that an ecumenical spirit is abroad it would seem of the utmost importance that trainees do not emerge from their courses with blinkered minds and no knowledge of therapeutic traditions other than the one in which they have been immersed. What is more, there needs to be a thorough study of those ethical and other professional issues which concern all counsellors, whatever their theoretical 'stable'.

Counselling does not take place in a vacuum and a training course needs to acknowledge this by drawing on relevant social science disciplines in order to illuminate the systems in which people live. Social, cultural, ethnic and political issues are but some of the ingredients of the kind of exploration which is required if justice is to be done to the study of the environment which in its different ways may profoundly affect the lives of clients. Nor can it be taken for granted that every trainee has a clear understanding of human development and the nature of the human personality. Some counselling theories explicitly incorporate such conceptualizations but there is again a strong case for presenting contrasting models so that trainees can wrestle with the combined and perhaps conflicting insights offered by biology, psychology, sociology and theology. In short, a counselling course which travels so light on academic content that it fails to do justice to at least some of the issues raised above is scarcely equipping its trainees for the kind of discourse which may well be demanded of them both by potential clients and by colleagues in allied disciplines.

**The course ethos and philosophical consistency**

Part of the discomfort that some counselling courses based in educational institutions have experienced arises from the ethos of competition, assessment and evaluation which not uncommonly prevails in such places and which, if anything, has grown more pronounced in recent years. Such an ethos is not conducive to the creation of a climate for learning where trainees can begin to take risks which inevitably render them vulnerable to the scrutiny and judgement of others. Central to most counselling approaches is a deep respect for the client and a willingness to understand and accept him or her without adverse judgement. If trainees themselves experience from their trainers attitudes and behaviours which are grossly at variance with such a philosophy of respect and acceptance it is likely that they will become angry and disillusioned at such a blatant discrepancy, and will justifiably suspect trainers of irresponsible inconsistency or, at worst, of manifest hypocrisy.

There are important issues here which have a bearing on almost every aspect of a training programme. Trainers are at all times models of the counselling approach which they represent and the way they lecture or facilitate small groups or conduct private interviews will be construed by trainees in the light of the practice and philosophy which they profess to advocate. This places a burden of expectation on the trainer which is not always easy to carry but there is no way in which this can be avoided. There can be few areas of vocational education where the credibility of the trainer is so much at stake in almost every word that is uttered and every action performed, however small and apparently inconsequential.

The issue of consistency may have profound implications for the way in which a course is structured. If, for example, the counselling approach which is being taught lays great emphasis on the trust-worthiness of the client and on his or her ability to discover inner resources, it makes little sense if the course structure is totally determined by the trainers in advance. It follows rather from the underlying theory that the trainees will increasingly be capable of discovering their own way forward and of generating their own resources. If opportunity is not provided for this kind of development then a glaring inconsistency rapidly becomes apparent. An even more sensitive area is likely to be the process of assessment and the methods employed for determining a student's eventual competence to practise. Courses where all the assessment power is retained in the hands of the trainers are unlikely to be in perfect harmony with the philosophy of the therapeutic approach which is being taught (unless perhaps it is a course in directive hypnosis!), and yet in some conventional institutions it may be inevitable, because of statutes and regulations, that boards of examiners retain the absolute power to pass or fail trainees. The tensions in situations like this can be unhealthy in the extreme and it may be incumbent on counsellor trainers to mount a concerted campaign on inappropriate institutional procedures with all the backing they can get from the British Association for Counselling and other professional bodies. That not all the blame can be placed on academic conservatism, however, is clearly evidenced by the fact that training courses run by private agencies and institutions are not always blameless when it comes to assessment procedures. The issues of power and status are complex and it is a formidable task to develop modes of evaluation which are at one and the same time sensitive to the trustworthiness of trainees, the insight and experience of trainers and the interests of future clients. The task is not impossible but it demands a level of honesty and humility which is seldom achieved in any profession. The appointment of an external consultant is almost certainly an essential ingredient in any process which is to stand much chance of evolving an assessment procedure which will be fully consistent with the underlying philosophy of the training which is being offered.

## Selection and resources

*Selection*
It may seem strange to leave the question of who should be accepted for counselling training to the final section of this discussion. Perhaps, however, the issue can be more realistically explored in the light of the course content and the demands of the training described above. The prospective trainee, it would seem, needs to be resourceful and resilient enough to embark upon a process which will require intense and continuing self-exploration, an ability to work with a range of clients, a willingness to participate fully in counselling skills work involving exposure to the scrutiny of others, a commitment to substantial academic study (often perfectly possible for those without high academic qualifications) and a preparedness to face almost inevitable disturbance and change in his or her personal life. This is a stiff challenge indeed and not one to be lightly undertaken.

The task faced by selectors is rendered the more difficult by the fact that almost all applicants are motivated and enthusiastic. What is more they often present as highly sensitive people with a genuine desire to help others. References can sometimes indicate areas which require further investigation but more often than not they reinforce this impression of a sensitive, thoughtful person with high motivation and well developed altruistic feelings. In the past some courses have employed personality tests or have set up somewhat daunting group situations where applicants can display their interpersonal skills in discussion with each other. There is little evidence to suggest that such methods are particularly successful. The issues which need to be explored are more difficult to get at for they are essentially to do with the applicant's state of readiness for the training experience. Such readiness is dependent upon the state of the person's internal and external world and both are notoriously difficult to explore in depth during a selection process. It would seem, however, that many would-be trainees are seeking a personal-growth experience rather than a training course and this is an issue which needs to be surfaced if at all possible. Not that it is usually a straightforward matter for clearly applicants who are not prepared to develop as persons during training are also unlikely candidates. The issue is one of balance and of priorities.

Related to the personal-growth issue is the appropriateness of enrolling students who are in personal therapy or have only recently finished a period of therapy. Clearly the experience of being a client is invaluable for a trainee and, as we have seen, there are many who believe that such an experience should be an integral part of training anyway. On the other hand, it is not unusual for those in therapy to be in a particularly vulnerable state or to be emerging from a period of considerable fragility or perturbation. Beginning on a training course may actually reopen wounds which are only just beginning to heal. As far as the external world is concerned it is not uncommon for applicants to be in difficult relationships (often marital) from which a training course promises an escape and the prospect of new persons with whom to relate more congenially. Some applicants, too, may be in difficult work situations where there is no job satisfaction and little prospect of improvement. Such factors are not automatically contra-indicators of suitability for training but they certainly raise a number of questions to which selectors need to be attentive. Candidates, too, who seem to have little support from their families and friends are likely to be at risk, as are those who have not thought through the implications of the energy, time and money involved in undertaking a training of such length and intensity. There is probably no fully satisfactory way of selecting trainees but it is certainly a process which requires the greatest of care and in which the candidate's world needs to be tapped beyond a superficial level. Certainly it should never be undertaken by one selector alone.

*Resources*

There can be few training roles as taxing as that of the counsellor trainer for he or she is likely to become deeply involved in the lives of many candidates who will be wrestling with major challenges in their personal and professional development. There are likely to be many crises of confidence among trainees and periods of confusion and debilitating self-doubt. Not only does the trainer have to be a sensitive companion to persons experiencing turmoil of this kind but he or she has also to perform the multiple tasks of the lecturer, group facilitator, skills trainer and scholarly academic. What is more, this kind of work has to be maintained at an intensive level over a lengthy period of time for no counselling course worthy of the name will be of shorter duration than one year full time or two to three years part time. One immediate implication of the demanding nature of the role is that counselling courses must have a high ratio of staff to students. No course should be run by one solitary individual and the core staff should probably be in the ratio of at least one to every eight to ten trainees. In addition there will clearly be a need for a range of supervision opportunities which may well involve many more staff. It is unlikely, too, that a small core staff will be able to cover adequately between them all aspects of the desirable curriculum and it is likely that several guest lecturers and tutors will have to be engaged at different stages. It goes without saying that core staff members should themselves be practising counsellors for there can be few occupations where the continuing interaction between practice and theory is of such fundamental importance in the training process. The trainer who is no longer practising as a counsellor will quickly lose the immediacy of experience which provides the major stimulus for creativity and is the principal source of his or her credibility in the eyes of trainees.

Counselling courses make heavy demands on staff time and energy and the sheer number of staff required, if effective supervision is to be provided, inevitably means that staff salaries will make considerable inroads on institutional budgets or on students' own financial resources where courses do not receive institutional subsidy. There seems to be no way round this unfortunate situation, which suggests that counselling training of high quality may well already have become inaccessible to those without substantial financial resources. It is to be hoped that some institutions at least will find it possible to make generous subsidies for counselling training and that charitable foundations will be increasingly prepared to support trainees without the necessary financial resources. If this does not prove to be so, the counselling world will undoubtedly be deprived of many gifted practitioners, especially from the ethnic minority groups in this country.

Apart from staff, the resource requirements of counselling courses are modest. There is a need for comfortable and flexible accommodation where it is comparatively easy to switch from one-to-one to small-group to large-group activities. For most therapeutic orientations training will be much enhanced by the ready availability of video and audio equipment and there is no escape from the fact that a reputable library is a *sine qua non*. Furthermore, in a field where changes are often rapid and where innovation can occur in unexpected quarters it is highly desirable that there is ready access to at least some of the leading professional journals. When all is said and done, however, the chief resource for every trainee remains the trainer. It is this person who by his or her integrity and skill will enable the trainee to move from timorous beginnings to the humble confidence of the fledgling counsellor. Perhaps in the last analysis the key issue which surpasses all the others in importance is the nature of the man or woman who is bold enough to undertake a task where success ultimately depends not simply on knowledge or even on experience but on a quality of being which can continue to offer support at those moments when the trainee is on the point of abandoning the struggle to enter so impossible a profession.

## Reference

British Association for Counselling (1988) *Recognition of Counselling Training Courses*. Rugby.

# 2 Approaches to the Training of Counsellors

## Windy Dryden and Brian Thorne

### Introduction

In the previous chapter we argued that initial counselling training courses should provide trainees with learning opportunities in four main areas: (a) self-exploration; (b) supervised work with clients; (c) the acquisition of counselling skills; and (d) counselling theory and relevant academic material. In this chapter we will discuss *how* this might be done and our focus then will be on *approaches* to initial counsellor training.

However, before embarking on a detailed discussion of these issues, we wish to make the following four points which the reader should bear in mind throughout the chapter. First, the four areas that we have outlined above are not discrete. Rather, they should be seen as interrelated components of a course's curriculum. While work with clients should be the central concern of any course designed to train counselling *practitioners*, the success of this is predicated on the following: (a) that trainees bring *themselves* to the work and as such they should be aware of and have an opportunity to overcome ways in which their personal agendas may interfere with effective counselling; (b) that counselling is a skilful enterprise and that effective counselling skills need to be acquired and internalized; and (c) that effective counsellors are guided by appropriate theoretical frameworks and salient knowledge (for example, of client problems).

Indeed, even the seemingly unrelated areas of theoretical knowledge and self-exploration are in fact crucially linked and thus trainees should be given opportunities to explore the personal implications of academic material. For example, if the research literature on anger is the focus of academic study, trainees should be encouraged to reflect on their own experience of being angry and explore both how this experience can be informed by research and how the research could possibly be illuminated or refuted by their experience.

Secondly, the choice of methods of training depends crucially upon the goals of that training. Furthermore, the goals of counsellor training will be inextricably linked with the trainers' view of the effective practitioner. Thus, on a person-centred counselling training course, the effective practitioner is one who is able to offer clients consistently high levels of the three core facilitative conditions – namely, empathy, acceptance and genuineness. The goal of such a course then would be to 'graduate' trainees who are able to do this and the question of training-method then becomes '*How* can we best help students to respond genuinely to clients with empathy and acceptance?'

A third point to be borne in mind is that the choice of methods of training counsellors will also depend upon who determines the curriculum. There are some counselling courses which are founded on the concept of self-directed learning. The philosophy that underpins such courses postulates that since effective counselling provides an environment where clients can direct their own learning, effective training should provide the same type of environment for trainees. Thus, trainees on such courses are encouraged to set their own learning objectives and choose how these objectives can best be met. It is likely that experiential methods will be used more frequently on such courses than on those where the curriculum is determined more by trainers than trainees, this being a situation which often prevails when the latter are validated by academic institutions.

Fourthly and finally, there is increasing evidence that effective counselling occurs when there is a strong working alliance between client and counsellor (see Dryden, 1989). This alliance has three major components: bonds, goals and tasks. Extrapolating from this evidence our hypothesis is that successful training depends on a strong working alliance between trainers and trainees (and indeed among trainees themselves). When trainers use alliance theory to inform their approach to training, a number of questions become salient. For example (a) can trainees see how participating in a particular training method (task) will lead to the achievement of their own training objectives (goal)?; (b) to what extent are trainees' training goals congruent with the training goals of the course?; and (c) what is the quality of the relationship (bond) between trainers and trainees and among trainees themselves and how does this affect trainees' engagement with and learning from their tasks as trainees?

While our emphasis in this chapter is on the task domain of counsellor training, the other two domains of the alliance should always be borne in mind when counsellor training *as a whole* is being considered. In particular our view is that the success of counsellor training is intimately related to the quality of the relationship between trainees and trainers (a point underscored by Shohet and Wilmot in their discussion of supervision – see Chapter 6). It is also clear that the assessment processes employed during a course may have major implications for this relationship, as indeed for much else within the training experience (see Chapter 3).

Having made the above points we will now consider how counsellor training may be approached in the four areas outlined at the beginning of the chapter. We will be particularly concerned with the advantages and disadvantages of the methods discussed.

**Self-exploration**

As we pointed out in the previous chapter (pp. 3–4) 'an unaware counsellor leading an unexamined life is likely to be a liability rather than an asset' as a practitioner. Indeed, there is some research evidence to suggest that client outcome is positively associated with lack of emotional disturbance in the counsellor (Beutler et al., 1986). How, then, do counsellor training courses formally encourage trainee self-exploration? We say formally here because we do, of course, recognize that trainee personal growth can and does take place through informal contact with trainers and fellow trainees.

*Personal therapy*
A traditional approach to trainee self-exploration has been to have trainees engage in their own personal therapy either as a requirement for course participation or as a valued but voluntary additional activity. This approach is particularly embraced by psychodynamically oriented counsellor trainers whose view is that trainee counsellors need to be acutely aware of their own personal dynamics so that they can distinguish between healthy and unhealthy countertransference reactions to their clients (Jacobs, 1988).

Courses vary in the degree of freedom they give trainees concerning their choice of personal therapist, varying from offering total freedom to providing trainees with a list of 'acceptable' therapists. This raises the issue of whether the orientation of trainees' personal therapists should be congruent with the orientation of the course. On balance, we think that such congruence is advantageous, otherwise trainees may become overly confused by the possible discrepancy between what they are being taught about counselling on their course and what they are learning about counselling from their personal therapy.

However, given that research has shown that 33 per cent of trainees have unsatisfactory personal-therapy experiences (Aveline, 1990), trainees should be encouraged to delay commitment to personal therapy until they have found a therapist with whom they feel they can work productively. This means that trainers should encourage trainees to 'shop around' until they have found a therapist who has a high degree of empathy with the likely experiences of trainee counsellors during the duration of their course. This, however, should *not* be a member of the training staff. In our opinion, when trainers serve as personal therapists to their trainees the fact that the latter will be evaluated in other areas of the course by the former does not ordinarily assist the creation of the best climate for fostering self-exploration. (Also, it is in violation of the BAC Code of Ethics and Practice for Trainers: see Appendix).

An important issue arises when the focus of trainees' personal therapy is considered. Should trainees allow themselves full rein to discuss whatever they choose in their personal therapy or should the focus be on the experiences and implications of being a trainee? While the former is the norm, it is worth experimenting with the latter. This might be one way to boost the correlation between personal therapy and therapist effectiveness, for at present there is equivocal evidence that having personal therapy improves one's effectiveness as a counsellor or therapist (Aveline, 1990).

*Personal development groups*
A common feature of many counsellor training courses is the personal development group (PDG) which is offered either in addition to personal therapy or instead of it. The major advantage of PDGs over personal therapy is that they offer trainees an opportunity to explore their relationships with one another and to benefit from the curative factors that groups provide (for example, universality, cohesion and interpersonal feedback). In particular, they provide a forum for the airing and resolution of interpersonal conflict among trainees which may otherwise spill over to other parts of the course and thereby inhibit learning.

The major disadvantage of PDGs is that they may not be the best forum for self-exploration for all trainees. Some trainees, like some clients, require the individual attention that the area of individual counselling provides (Dryden, 1991).

The effective leader of PDGs should (a) be an experienced group facilitator; (b) be sensitive to the needs and stage of personal development of trainee counsellors; (c) have a therapeutic orientation congruent with that of the course; and (d) should not be involved in the formal evaluation of trainees.

We have argued that trainees' personal therapists and PDG leaders should ideally be unconcerned with the formal evaluation of trainees. It goes without saying that these therapists/leaders should maintain confidentiality with respect to their trainee clients.

Whether or not their confidentiality should be absolute is debatable. There is a case for a course leader being alerted to the fact that a trainee is severely distressed and perhaps potentially harmful to clients. Frequently, trainees will realize this themselves and, with or without prompting from their therapist, discuss the situation with their tutor. On the rare occurrence where a trainee refuses to acknowledge this state of affairs, the therapist or PDG leader may choose to break confidentiality and inform the course tutor in order to safeguard the welfare of the trainees' clients. If this is going to be the case trainees need to be informed of the limits of confidentiality in advance.

*Journal work*
It is now common practice for trainees to be asked to keep personal journals of their experiences on their training courses. What varies among courses is the amount of structure the participants are given within which to explore these experiences. Some tutors formally train students in intense journal methods (for example, Progoff, 1975), while others broadly explain the purpose of keeping such journals (i.e. to explore and reflect upon personal and professional development) and give minimal specific guidance on how this might be done or what might be covered.

If trainers respect individual differences concerning the form of a journal (for example, some trainees prefer to keep a verbal record on audio-tape) and if trainees engage in this task regularly, it can be a powerful stimulus for private reflection and self-exploration. In particular it is a helpful format for setting and reviewing training objectives. However, some trainees require the presence of another person to engage meaningfully in self-exploration and for these the tape-recording of co-counselling sessions (when the trainee is the client) can be a valuable alternative. Other trainees may be constrained by the knowledge that their tutors will have access to their journals and thus on some courses it is a requirement that journals be kept but they do not have to be handed in for appraisal.

While personal therapy, PDGs and journal work are the main approaches to fostering trainee self-exploration on counselling training courses, several other methods are commonly employed which we will now briefly note.

*Other approaches*

*Peer counselling*  Here trainees counsel one another for an agreed time period in a co-counselling format (Evison and Horobin, 1988). This can be done within or outside the context of counsellor skills training. While this should never be the only form of self-exploration on a course it can be very helpful where the trainees concerned trust each other. It is less helpful when that trust is lacking and where one or both trainees have poorly developed counselling skills.

*Personal tutorials*    Unless a training course is particularly well endowed with staff it is unlikely that trainees will receive many individual personal tutorials. When they do occur they can provide a very useful format for tutors and trainees to explore the latter's personal and professional development. If the trainee respects the tutor and the tutor offers both positive feedback and suggestions for future development this can be the stimulus for healthy self-exploration and growth. However, when the tutor just gives negative feedback this can be very discouraging for the trainee.

While courses should ideally provide regular opportunities for trainees to give feedback on their experiences of the course (usually in a group setting), the personal tutorial can also be used for eliciting individual trainee feedback. When this is non-defensively received and taken seriously, it can foster in the trainee the empowering feeling that he or she can have an influence on the course's future development.

*Community and residential meetings*    On many training programmes opportunities are provided for the course to meet regularly as a community and occasionally in a residential setting for an extended time period. Whether or not the stated purpose of such meetings is for personal growth, there is no doubt that, although often anxiety provoking, such experiences can have a powerful positive effect on trainees. However, if unskilfully led, such meetings also have the potential to be damaging, particularly if scapegoating is allowed to occur unchecked.

In closing, and as noted at the beginning of this chapter, the major areas of training are interdependent. As such, much useful self-exploration can be initiated in the skills, supervision and academic components of training courses if trainees are given the time and opportunity to reflect on the personal implications of what is learned in these other contexts.

## Supervised work with clients

We argued at the beginning of this chapter that work with clients forms the central core of courses designed to train counselling practitioners. It follows that regular supervision of this work is crucial. However, the success of this supervision depends upon a number of factors. First, trainees need to be deemed ready to see clients. Thus, before seeing clients, trainees need to demonstrate an emerging capacity to (a) respond consistently to clients from the latter's frame of reference; (b) communicate empathic understanding of clients' concerns; (c) be genuine and non-defensive in their interactions with clients; (d) demonstrate unconditional acceptance of their clients; (e) maintain appropriate confidentiality; and (f) demonstrate a working knowledge of severe psychopathology so that they can refer on clients who can be better served by other therapeutic intervention. It is likely that much initial work in counselling skills groups and personal development groups will be devoted to preparing trainees to demonstrate 'readiness' on these criteria.

Secondly, successful supervision depends upon a good working alliance being established between the trainee, the agency where the trainee will see clients and the training course. For example, if the course requires the trainee to tape-record his or her counselling sessions (with, of course, the agreement of the client), the trainee needs to accept this (before entering the course). In addition, the agency needs to give permission for this to happen before the placement begins. Thus, a productive channel of communication between the trainee, the course tutor and the agency needs to be established and maintained throughout the time that the trainee is on placement. If problems do arise during the placement, there also has to be a forum in which such problems can be discussed and resolved.

Thirdly, appropriate selection of clients to be counselled by trainees needs to be undertaken which takes into account the stage of development reached by each trainee as a counsellor.

Fourthly, the counselling orientation of supervisors needs to be congruent with the orientation of the course. Supervision can be doomed from the outset if, for example, a psychodynamic supervisor is assigned to a trainee who is being trained in cognitive-behavioural counselling.

Having outlined the above preconditions for effective supervision we will now consider how such supervision may be approached. To avoid duplication we will not consider material discussed by Hawkins and Shohet in Chapter 7. We will thus consider supervision methods which focus on what *actually* goes on in counselling sessions and methods which focus on *discussion* of what goes on in counselling sessions.

*The 'actual data' approach to supervision*
When the focus of supervision is on what actually goes on between trainee counsellor and client, the supervisor needs access to an

accurate record of this interaction. While psychodynamic super-visors often encourage and train their supervisees to take detailed verbatim 'process notes' immediately after counselling sessions, this method has not been shown to provide a reliable record of the interaction (Covner, 1944; Muslin et al., 1981). Thus use of audio recordings, video recordings with an audio channel or live inter-views are necessary if actual data are to be obtained.

When audio and video recordings form the basis of supervision the focus is frequently on how trainees actually respond to client material. Feedback can be given to trainees concerning verbal and non-verbal interventions that are both helpful and unhelpful. With respect to the latter, trainees can be encouraged to consider alternative interventions which could have been more enabling.

In addition, the review of audio and video recordings in supervi-sion can provide a structure for discussion of the trainee's experi-ences at various stages of the interview. Methods such as Interper-sonal Process Recall (see Kagan, 1984) and Brief Structured Recall (see Elliott and Shapiro, 1988) can be of additional use here. When such recordings are used in this way the focus of supervision often changes to a discussion of what went on in the session.

Audio and video recordings can also be used to discuss what the trainee intended by a particular response (Hill and O'Grady, 1985). What the supervisor does here is to stop the tape after every verbal response made by the trainee, who is asked to recall what he or she intended by the response. (See Dryden, 1984: 358 for a list of therapist intentions. This list can be given to trainees to stimulate recall.)

The advantage of the use of audio and video recordings in supervision is that they allow the supervisor access to what actually went on in a session and thus permit him or her to give trainees feedback concerning actual interventions made. They are then best used when the focus of supervision is on specific counselling responses and on the skill element of counselling.

Such recordings are often used by supervisors who embrace person-centred (and other humanistic approaches), Transactional Analysis and cognitive-behavioural counselling, but are not used frequently by psychodynamic supervisors whose concern is much more on understanding the dynamics of what goes on in counselling.

The disadvantages of such methods is that supervisors can easily get bogged down in micro issues to the neglect of macro issues such as understanding the client and the dynamics of the counsellor–client relationship, treatment planning and case management. Addi-tionally, the use of such methods often leads to trainees becoming self-conscious, a phenomenon which usually disappears with their continued use. However, for such trainees and those with acute performance anxiety their use is contra-indicated until this anxiety can be reduced (see Dryden, 1987).

Live supervision is a method that requires the supervisor to watch and listen to the trainee conducting an actual counselling session (with the client's informed consent) while being able to talk to the trainee via a 'bug in the ear', giving immediate feedback on the counselling and making suggestions for possible intervention. The main advantages of this method lie in the fact that immediate feedback can be given and that trainees can immediately implement their supervisors' suggestions and monitor the effects of their interventions. Its main disadvantage lies in the fact that it can be unduly distracting for both the counsellor and client.

*The case discussion approach to supervision*
In case discussion[1] the supervisory focus is precisely on those issues which 'actual data' methods tend to neglect. The emphasis here is more on macro than micro counselling issues. Discussion tends to centre on understanding the client and understanding the relationship between counsellor and client from a broader perspective than can be achieved with 'actual data' supervision methods. In addition, treatment planning and case management issues are frequently the focus of concern in case discussion. As mentioned above, psychodynamic supervisors make much use of this supervision approach, focusing particularly on possible unconscious factors that influence the counselling and on issues of transference and countertransference.

Case discussion supervisors differ concerning how much structure they encourage trainees to bring to the discussion (for an example of a structured approach to case discussion see Jacobs, 1981). They all, however, tend to stress the possible presence of parallel process where the dynamics of the supervisor–trainee interaction may parallel the dynamics of the trainee counsellor–client interaction (see Shohet and Wilmot, Chapter 6 and McNeill and Worthen, 1989).

The major disadvantage of case discussion as an approach to supervision is that it cannot focus on what *actually* transpired in the counselling session. Thus it is not an appropriate method if the focus of concern is on counselling skills.

The reader will probably have anticipated our conclusion – namely, that we advocate the use of *both* case discussion *and* 'actual data' approaches to supervision. The important task of the supervisor here is to use the approach that is best suited to the focus of concern being addressed at any point in the supervisory relationship. To encourage trainees to see the value of *both* these approaches, it is very helpful for supervisors to discuss occasionally one or two of their own cases and to play tapes from these cases (if indeed they make them).

**Training in counselling skills**

Attempts to demystify the process of counselling so that researchers could study the relationship between counsellor behaviour and client outcome began in earnest with the publication of Truax and Carkhuff's (1967) seminal work. These authors developed scales which detailed, more than anyone had done previously, specific features of the core conditions of counsellor empathy, unconditional positive regard and congruence. This landmark work spawned a number of similar (but not identical) approaches to conceptualize counselling as a process at different points during which counsellors require different skills. Furthermore, the originators of these approaches (for example, Carkhuff, 1987; Egan, 1990; Ivey, 1988) developed training 'packages' designed to train counsellors in these skills.

These skills training 'packages' stress three main phases of skilled counsellor activity – to facilitate exploration, understanding and action. They thus all have their roots in the client-centred tradition but in their different ways have added other phases and skills not emphasized by this approach. As mentioned above they all tried to break down broad counselling processes into teachable and learnable skills although they vary concerning the degree to which they specify these skills (see Larson, 1984, and Baker et al., 1990 for a fuller discussion of these and other skills training 'packages').

Before describing how such skills may be taught let us consider some advantages and disadvantages of skills training. If skills training is considered as one interdependent part of the entire training process then it can be a very useful way of encouraging trainees (a) to distinguish between helpful and unhelpful ways of responding to clients and (b) to make helpful responses in a clear and effective manner.

However, if skills training is seen as the only approach to counsellor education or if it is given undue importance in the curriculum then there is a danger that trainees may become good technicians without having the opportunity to examine their attitudes towards themselves, others and the world. Thus the relationship between skills training and self-exploration work, in particular, is a delicate one that needs careful monitoring. Just as we do not wish to train good but unaware technicians we also do not wish to train aware but poor communicators. Both endeavours are important and are intertwined.

If we take the view that breaking down broad descriptions of effective counselling into more discrete counselling skills is a worthwhile activity[2] and that these skills can be taught and learned then *how* can this be done? Carkhuff (1969) made the important point that there are two major elements to effective counsellor communication. The first involves good discrimination skills; i.e. trainee counsellors need to be able to discriminate (a) between accurate and inaccurate formulations of what clients communicate and (b) between helpful and unhelpful counsellor responses to these communications. Thus, before being able to respond effectively to clients, trainees need to be accurate in their understanding of what their clients are experiencing and what might constitute helpful responses to this experiencing. Exercises designed to sharpen trainees' discrimination skills include the presentation of client statements either on audio, video or in written form, along with a number of options which (a) detail accurate and inaccurate representations of the client's experience and, later, (b) helpful and unhelpful counsellor responses (with respect to the target skill) to that experience. Trainees then have to choose an option that best represents the client's experience and the most helpful counsellor response. Discussion follows which usually centres on the basis for the trainees' choices.

When trainees demonstrate adequate discrimination on a particular skill the emphasis shifts to the second major element, namely effective responding in using the target skill (see below).

A somewhat related way of considering counselling skills training is to look at it as a process. Based on Ford's (1979) excellent research review of this area we can conceptualize this process as involving (a) instruction; (b) modelling; (c) practice; and (d) feedback. We will now briefly consider each in turn and will assume that skills are to be taught one at a time.

*Instruction*
Instruction is used throughout the skills training process but is particularly salient at the outset in both a general and specific sense. In the general sense, at the beginning of a skills training group the tutor will explain verbally and with reference to handouts and set texts the overall model of skills training to be employed during this component of the training course. This model may be one already in existence, an amalgam of what is available or one devised by the tutor. Whichever approach is used it is important that trainees are

given an overall picture of the model and its purpose and have an opportunity to discuss it before specific skills are introduced.

When specific skills are introduced, instructions (where the skill is explained and its purpose and limits thoroughly discussed) are helpful before modelling is introduced.

*Modelling*
After a skill has been introduced and explained many tutors (but not all) present a good model of the skill to be learned. Ford (1979) notes that there are three issues with respect to this modelling: (a) the model; (b) the message; and (c) the medium.

With respect to the *model*, it is likely that a coping model (i.e. good enough but not perfect) is more helpful than one which shows flawless performance (the mastery model) in encouraging trainees to practise the skill with confidence. Mastery models can lead trainees to feel hopeless about learning the skill while coping models are more credible for trainees and tend to inspire hope. It is for this reason that flawless live performances by tutors and by master counsellors on videotape have their limitations as effective models, at least until trainees have internalized the target skill.

With respect to the *message*, it is important, as noted above, that demonstration of effective *and* ineffective examples of the skill be modelled so that trainees can learn to discriminate accurately before being expected to respond effectively. If audio or video models are portrayed, relevant cues (for example, audible tones or captions) need to be used if trainees are to be helped to recognize the skill if it is embedded in counselling interactions where other skills may be demonstrated.

With respect to the *medium*, models can be live, shown on videotape, heard on audio tape or presented in written form. Obviously the target skill will determine to a large extent the medium used (for example, non-verbal skills require live or video-taped demonstration).

We mentioned earlier that not all tutors use modelling at this stage of the skills training process. Such tutors fear that exposure to models at this point might lead trainees to imitate the model rather than integrate the skill into their natural style of responding. Thus, such tutors proceed directly from instruction to practice and use modelling at a later stage of the counselling skills training process.

*Practice*
When trainees are given an opportunity to practise the skill under consideration there are different ways in which this can be done.

Perhaps the most frequently used approach is to use 'peer counselling' where one trainee counsels a fellow trainee for a period of time. The question which then arises concerns whether the trainee client discusses a real concern or adopts the role of a client and invents a problem. The main advantage of the 'real problem' situation is that the 'client' is referring to his or her own real feelings during the counselling and can give reliable feedback to the counsellor concerning the impact of the skill under consideration. Also, the 'client' can be successfully helped to explore a significant issue by the peer 'counsellor', showing them both that trainees can be helpful in the counselling role. The main disadvantage is that the client may go further in his or her exploration of the concern than anticipated and become quite distressed as a result. In such cases the amount and quality of support present on the course is a crucial factor in determining the impact of this situation on the distressed trainee. In many respects, trainers are responsible for creating a 'holding' environment for their trainees. An obvious but sometimes neglected maxim here is 'put the welfare of the trainee before skills practice' if the two conflict. However, if the skills group is the only forum in which trainees can explore themselves, this blurring of the boundaries is inevitable with dubious results. In such cases, trainees will neither have sufficient time for learning skills, nor adequate opportunity to explore concerns in depth and at length.

The disadvantage of role-playing a client in skills practice is that the 'client' can either abandon the role in an attempt to be a 'good' client for his or her colleague or may stick rigidly to the role, negating any helpful shift in experience as a result of counselling. It is a skill in itself to portray accurately a role with the right degree of flexibility. This is why some courses on occasion employ actors to play the role of clients. On the other hand, the main advantage of role-playing is that it not only safeguards the welfare of trainees but later in the course the 'client' trainee can play the role of his or her own clients and learn more about the latter, sometimes with great immediacy.

Other approaches to skills practice involve responding to brief written audio taped or videotaped 'client' vignettes and the use of actors (as noted above). Rarely, if ever, are genuine clients used in counselling skills groups.

*Feedback*
Trainees will best learn and refine their counselling skills if they are given feedback. Ford (1979) has noted that there are four issues with respect to feedback: (a) the message; (b) feedback valence; (c) the medium; and (d) the source.

With respect to the *message*, feedback may be a simple 'right' or 'wrong' response or it may include information which (a) encourages greater discrimination, (b) provides greater explanation than had been given hitherto, and (c) involves the use of modelling. The main research finding concerning the message component of feedback is that performance-specific feedback is more effective than non-specific feedback in aiding the acquisition of the target counselling skill (Ford, 1979).

The *valence* of the feedback ranges from positive to negative in kind or more neutral informational feedback. Our experience is that judiciously given positive feedback with specific information and instructions concerning future improvement is the type found most useful by trainees although this area needs to be researched. Consistent negative feedback is destructive and demoralizing, consistent positive feedback has a Pollyannish quality to it which leads trainees to doubt the sincerity of the feedback source, while consistent neutral (informational) feedback leaves trainees wondering about how well or poorly they are performing.

Concerning the *medium* of feedback, this is usually verbal although written feedback is also used by tutors in interim or final evaluations of trainee performance in skills groups. The use of numerical feedback is also appropriate if the tutor is using scales (such as Carkhuff's (1969) five-point scales of counsellor functioning) to indicate a range of skill levels.

Also, if feedback is to be given, the source of the feedback needs direct access to skill performance. One way is through live observation. Here feedback can be given at the end of an observed sequence, or during it (either through the use of bug-in-the-ear devices or when the source interrupts the sequence to make a point). How and when feedback is given in this respect can vary according to the trainee's preference.

Feedback can also be given in response to audio-taped or video-taped counselling sessions, video being particularly useful when non-verbal skills are salient. However, trainees will need to become comfortable using these media while counselling before benefiting fully from such feedback.

Finally the *source* of the feedback can be the tutor, the trainee client, an observer (if counselling triads are used) or the trainee counsellor who gives feedback to himself or herself. All four are best used in rotation unless this becomes confusing for the trainee. If tutor feedback alone is given, this communicates that trainees' views are unimportant, while if only trainees' feedback is used the expertise of the tutor is not utilized. Here, as elsewhere in counsellor training, a healthy balance should be the objective.

Before leaving this discussion of skills training we would like to stress that other methods can be used to add a useful dimension to the emphasis on skills. Thus Interpersonal Process Recall (IPR) methods (Kagan, 1984) can be very helpful during skills training to elucidate the covert and often difficult-to-identify elements of 'counsellor' or 'client' experience, for example, during skills practice sessions. Here the tutor (or someone else) replays the tape of the counselling, encouraging 'counsellor' or 'client' to stop the tape whenever they want to discuss an important experience felt during the counselling and recalled by listening to the tape. This experiential element often sheds light on the session which might otherwise be neglected due to the emphasis on observable skills. While IPR should not be used exclusively in skills training since it was not designed to facilitate skill acquisition (Baker et al., 1990; Kagan and Kagan, 1990), it can be usefully employed as an adjunct in skills training to tease out relevant covert experiences which need to be processed *along with* the focus on observable skills.

We have concentrated here on the acquisition of discrete skills. Similar remarks can be made concerning how integration of skills can be approached although this is a complex issue and beyond the scope of this chapter. Suffice it to say, the development of skill integration is a slow process in which supervision of casework plays a central role.

**Theory and academic work**

Counselling theory and related academic work is all too frequently the poor relation on counselling courses. Many trainees have vivid past memories of sitting passively while academics deliver lectures on topics that could easily be read in books. In the previous chapter we made the case for this element of counselling training and note here that how it is approached often determines the degree to which trainees value theoretical and academic material.

*Lectures*
Counselling trainees, in general, will not tolerate a course where lectures are the predominant way in which knowledge is communicated, and neither should they have to do so. However, lectures do have their place on a counselling course. In our view lectures should be given to outline a framework within which subsequent theoretical/academic material can be best understood. Also, well delivered lectures on topics not easily accessible in written form are usually well appreciated by students. In both these cases, however,

the lecturer should give trainees plenty of time to discuss and ask questions about the presented material.

*Seminars*
When academic material is easily accessible in written form seminars can be usefully held to discuss matters arising from this material. The success of these seminars depends upon (a) trainees undertaking to read the material before the seminar is held; (b) a list of discussion items being presented well in advance of the seminar; and (c) someone, either a tutor or trainee, leading the discussion in a focused way, encouraging participants to keep to the theme of the seminar. On this latter point, if trainees are to lead effective seminars they will need guidance on how they can best do so; otherwise trainee-led seminars can easily degenerate into lectures given by the trainee. This also happens when fellow trainees have not read the material in advance. To prevent this from happening, readings need to be focused and manageable given the constraints of time and the other demands that the course places on trainees. On some courses learning contracts are made which specify what trainees agree to read and as long as the amount of reading is manageable these contracts can be effective. However, unless the contracts are made in a spirit of negotiation, trainees may experience them as coercive.

The size of the seminar group is another important variable in determining the success of seminars. In our experience 13–14 trainees is the absolute maximum number for a seminar group where productive debate and discussion can take place and groups of eight or nine are preferable.

*Tutorials*
In these days of deteriorating staff–student ratios it is unlikely that courses in institutions of further and higher education will be able to offer students regular individual or small-group academic tutorials. This is a pity since this approach to academic work can be very stimulating for both tutor and trainee. At a minimum, however, each trainee should have one individual tutorial per term in which the trainee's academic development is discussed along with his or her progress in the three other elements discussed in this chapter.

*Projects*
Much useful collaborative academic work can be done by a group of trainees electing to study a particular area or facet of counselling, to prepare the material and to present this to the rest of the course.

This approach is particularly well utilized by courses which are organized around the principle of self-directed learning.

Whichever teaching or learning methods are used, however, academic work should not be isolated from the rest of the curriculum and our previous remarks concerning the interrelated nature of the four elements discussed in this chapter bear one final reiteration.

## Notes

1 See Chapter 7 by Hawkins and Shohet for a discussion of group vs. individual supervision.
2 Not all counsellor trainers take this view. In particular psychodynamic trainers tend to place less emphasis on skills training, focusing more on the blocks to effective communication.

## References

Aveline, M.O. (1990) 'The training and supervision of individual therapists', in W. Dryden (ed.), *Individual Therapy: A Handbook*. Milton Keynes: Open University Press.

Baker, S.B., Daniels, T.G. and Greeley, A. (1990) 'Systematic training of graduate-level counselors: narrative and meta-analytic reviews of three major programs', *Counseling Psychologist*, 18: 355–421.

Beutler, L.E., Crago, M. and Arizmendi, T.G. (1986) 'Research on therapist variables in psychotherapy', in S.L. Garfield and A.E. Bergin (eds), *Handbook of Psychotherapy and Behavior Change*, 3rd edition. New York: Wiley.

Carkhuff, R.R. (1969) *Helping and Human Relations: A Primer for Lay and Professional Helpers* (vols 1 and 2). New York: Holt, Rinehart & Winston.

Carkhuff, R.R. (1987) *The Art of Helping VI*. Amherst, Mass.: Human Resource Development Press.

Covner, B.J. (1944) 'Studies in phonographic recordings of verbal material: III. The completeness and accuracy of counseling interview reports', *Journal of General Psychology*, 30: 181–203.

Dryden, W. (ed.) (1984) *Individual Therapy in Britain*. Milton Keynes: Open University Press.

Dryden, W. (1987) *Current Issues in Rational-Emotive Therapy*. Beckenham, Kent: Croom Helm.

Dryden, W. (1989) 'The therapeutic alliance as an integrating framework', in W. Dryden (ed.), *Key Issues for Counselling in Action*. London: Sage.

Dryden, W. (1991) *Dryden on Counselling. Volume 1: Seminal Papers*. London: Whurr Publishers.

Egan, G. (1990) *The Skilled Helper: A Systematic Approach to Effective Helping* (4th edition). Pacific Grove: Brooks/Cole.

Elliott, R. and Shapiro, D.A. (1988) 'Brief structured recall: a more efficient method for studying significant therapy events', *British Journal of Medical Psychology*, 61: 141–53.

Evison, R. and Horobin, R. (1988) 'Co-counselling', in J. Rowan and W. Dryden (eds), *Innovative Therapy in Britain*. Milton Keynes: Open University Press.

Ford, J.D. (1979) 'Research on training counselors and clinicians', *Review of Educational Research*, 49: 87–130.

Hill, C.E. and O'Grady, K.E. (1985) 'List of therapist intentions illustrated in a case study and with therapists of varying theoretical orientations', *Journal of Counseling Psychology*, 32: 3–22.

Ivey, A.E. (1988) *Intentional Interviewing and Counseling: Facilitating Client Development*. Pacific Grove: Brooks/Cole.

Jacobs, M. (1981) 'Setting the record straight', *Counselling*, 36: 10–13.

Jacobs, M. (1988) *The Presenting Past*. London: Harper & Row.

Kagan, N. (1984) 'Interpersonal process recall: basic methods and recent research', in D. Larson (ed.), *Teaching Psychological Skills: Models for Giving Psychology Away*. Monterey, Calif.: Brooks/Cole.

Kagan, N. and Kagan, H. (1990) 'IPR: a validated model for the 1990s and beyond', *Counseling Psychologist*, 18: 436–40.

Larson, D. (ed.) (1984) *Teaching Psychological Skills: Models for Giving Psychology Away*. Monterey, Calif.: Brooks/Cole.

McNeill, B.W. and Worthen, V. (1989) 'The parallel process in psychotherapy supervision', *Professional Psychology: Research and Practice*, 20: 329–33.

Muslin, H.L., Thurnblad, R.J. and Meschel, G. (1981) 'The fate of the clinical interview: an observational study', *American Journal of Psychiatry*, 138 (6): 825–33.

Progoff, I. (1975) *At a Journal Workshop*. New York: Dialogue House Library.

Truax, C.B. and Carkhuff, R.R. (1967) *Toward Effective Counseling and Psychotherapy: Training and Practice*. Chicago: Aldine.

# 3 Selection and Assessment in Counsellor Training Courses

## Campbell Purton

This chapter offers a survey of the approaches to selection and assessment adopted in four established counselling courses. My aim is to give a fairly full account of the procedures adopted in these courses, and at the same time to draw attention to how the differences between the approaches are related to the general philosophies informing the courses.

The four courses I discuss cover a range of counselling approaches – the psychodynamic, the person-centred, the eclectic and psychosynthesis. They are, respectively:

1 Diploma Course in Advanced Psychodynamic Counselling, organized by the Westminster Pastoral Foundation (I shall refer to this as the 'WPF course');
2 Training Course in Person-Centred Counselling and Psychotherapy, organized by the Facilitator Development Institute, Britain[1] (the 'FDI course');
3 University of London M.Sc. in Counselling, organized by Goldsmiths' College (the 'M.Sc. course');
4 Professional Training Course in Counselling and Psychotherapy, organized by the Psychosynthesis and Education Trust (the 'psychosynthesis course').

The factual material I present was obtained through interviews with staff members of the courses, as well as from course documents. The staff members were Paul Keeble for the WPF course, Brian Thorne for the FDI course, Windy Dryden for the M.Sc. course and Diana Whitmore for the psychosynthesis course.

Before looking at the details of selection and assessment in each of these courses, it may be useful to reflect on what principles in general could or should inform these procedures. What sort of assessment is appropriate for the very special kinds of training that are involved? What criteria are relevant in selecting trainees in the first place?

These questions raise a wide range of issues, some of which touch on deep questions about the general nature of counselling as a profession. Counselling is by definition a very individual and personal activity, yet the very conception of training involves something in the way of agreed standards of what counts as competence. A crucial issue with which any responsible training programme has to wrestle, then, is how to protect and encourage the development of the trainee's individual style, while providing adequate critical assessment. Similarly, a balance has to be found between encouraging trainees to learn from their own experience, and providing them with the opportunity to learn from the experience of others. And linked with this is the need to balance the requirement that a trainee should have some critical awareness of the theoretical perspectives underlying counselling practice, with the need of individual trainees to find their own perspective.

So far as selection is concerned it may be easiest to agree on what should count *against* selecting a particular candidate. I think that many of the doubts a selector might reasonably feel have to do with the candidate's motivation. It seems reasonable to exclude someone whose interest is of a casual nature, who is merely dabbling in counselling. All the courses discussed effectively discourage such applicants, simply through making sure that applicants are aware of the commitments they are taking on. Another fairly clear negative criterion for selection would be serious psychopathology in the applicant: the WPF course is particularly concerned about this issue, but each of the courses is clear that their function is the provision of training rather than therapy. Among other inappropriate motivations could be power-seeking, purely academic interest and the wish to belong to a counselling 'in-group'. In addition to these motivational considerations, which the different courses emphasize to different degrees, there are considerations of intellectual ability and emotional maturity, together with the applicant's resources in terms of time and money.

Regarding assessment the issues are more complex. There are issues to do with whether the trainee has come to acquire enough of 'what it takes to be a competent counsellor', in terms of skills, theoretical knowledge, self-knowledge, emotional sensitivity and so on. Some of these qualities are open to formal assessment, some less so. Then there are issues to do with whether the trainee is likely to cause harm to his or her clients, through over- or under-involvement, power-seeking, the satisfaction of unconscious needs at the client's expense and so on. The requirements of assessment in this connection are not easily met by any formal procedure. Rather, I think, they tend to be met through the general structure of a course, with its particular blend of self-, peer and staff assessment opportunities. The assessment procedures differ widely between the courses, and I shall say more about these differences after looking at the details of selection and assessment in each case.

One further preliminary point seems worth making. Counselling is generally accepted to be more of an art than a science, so that it is unreasonable to expect its professional training standards to be specifiable in a hard and fast way. As in many other professions, but to a greater degree, assessment must involve elements of intuition and personal judgement which may not always be easy to back up with argument. This will be especially true in justifying assessments to those working in different counselling traditions. To some extent counsellor training must involve something of an initiation into the tradition which is embodied in the training course, and whether the training results in a satisfactory outcome will depend partly on how the trainee is able to relate to the tradition to which he is exposed. Writing of therapy more generally, Joel Kovel remarks:[2]

> All therapies offer some sense of community . . . . Indeed a kind of communal feeling is established with the entire ideology and institution of the therapy, its way of life . . . . Whoever undertakes therapy, then, should recognize that he is going to experience a powerful pull towards joining up with its community, and that the kinds of feelings he is likely to find himself having towards the therapist and the therapeutic ideology are going to play a large role in what happens to him.

Whether or not this is always true of individual therapy, it does seem undeniably true of any extended counsellor training. Selection and assessment cannot be separated from this 'initiatory' element, so that although criteria of one sort or another can be usefully established, it remains true that selection involves something like offering a trainee the opportunity of 'becoming one of us', and assessment is to some extent the assessment of whether he or she has 'become one of us'. In the four courses reviewed here I think the initiatory element is probably strongest in the FDI and psychosynthesis courses, and least prominent in the M.Sc. course, but I believe it is a significant aspect of each course which should not be lost sight of in studying the details of the selection and assessment procedures.

**Selection**

*The WPF course*
WPF offers three routes to its Diploma which is awarded jointly with the Roehampton Institute of Higher Education: a two-year course, which is full time in the first year, a three-year half-time

course and a four-year day-release course. The general principles of selection and assessment are similar for each of these routes.

The selection process for the WPF course is lengthy and intensive. This is partly a consequence of the fact that trainees will begin to work with clients within three weeks of starting the course.

The general principles of selection are: (a) the candidate should have some experience of the helping relationship; there should be some evidence that they are able to listen, attend and so on; (b) there should be clear evidence of growing self-awareness, either through personal therapy or group interaction; and (c) they should have had at least one year of counselling skills training (WPF run an appropriate course, but other courses are acceptable).

More generally, the selection process is informed by a concern with both potential and pathology: 'Can this person learn?', but also 'How do they handle anxiety? Is there evidence of gross deficiency in their personal defences? Are they able to reflect on neurotic or psychotic aspects of themselves?' The psychodynamic nature of the WPF course is thus reflected in the considerations which inform the selection process, and the selection interviewers are required to work with unconscious as well as with conscious dimensions. This is seen as important since the trainee's basic stability may well be under threat when working with a very disturbed client.

In practice the selection process works as follows. There is a short application form. If the answers to the questions on this seem appropriate the applicant is asked to submit an account of their own life: an autobiographical case-study. Guidelines for this are given in the form of a questionnaire which includes references to early experience, relations with parents and so on. WPF may write to the applicant for further clarification. No applicants under the age of 25 or over 60 are interviewed; interviews are unlikely for those in the 25–30 and 55–60 age-groups. Two references are requested.

Candidates who appear promising are invited to a selection interview. The interview, lasting about 75 minutes, is conducted by one of WPF's senior therapists. The interviewer's brief is to look at what emerges in the interview, at how applicants handle their anxiety, for example. The interviewer submits a 1½ page report, including comments on countertransference feelings, and this report is made available to a selection committee (see below). On this basis the applicant is provisionally assessed as a probable/possible/ unlikely candidate.

Candidates are then invited to a half-day selection event. Normally sixteen people are invited, being divided into two groups of eight. The session divides into two halves. In the first half the applicants are given a page of information about a client. They are requested to discuss with the group and group supervisor how they would offer counselling to this client. The supervisor's role is partly to facilitate the discussion, but also to note how the applicants respond in a situation which can arouse considerable anxiety because of the elements of competition and concern over self-presentation. In the second half of the session the group is asked to explore and reflect on what has been happening in the group so far. A group facilitator sits with the group and assesses how the applicants use skills such as empathy, confrontation and coping with anxiety.

A selection committee of five or six staff meets immediately after the half-day event and the two WPF staff involved in the event give verbal reports. The report of the selection interview is studied, most weight being given to this in reaching the final decision. Rapid agreement is usually reached on the suitability of perhaps half of the applicants, and the others are discussed at length. Applicants' references may be taken into account at this stage, where the committee finds it difficult to reach agreement. Typical numbers involved would be: 150 initial applications, 80 full applications, 60 interviews, 40 half-day participants, 25 accepted.

*The FDI course*

This is a 2½ year part-time course leading to a diploma of the Facilitator Development Institute. The selection process for the course consists of the completion of an application form and a selection interview. Two references are required, and referees are given guidelines. The general considerations informing the selection process are: (a) evidence is sought that the applicant has a sufficient level of sophistication in self-awareness and self-exploration to make it likely that they will be able to complete the course without becoming hopelessly tangled in their own psychological difficulties; (b) evidence is sought that the applicant has already undertaken some helping activity which requires an empathic capacity; (c) it is important that applicants should have some knowledge of what the person-centred approach involves, and that they should be choosing this course on the basis of such knowledge.

The application form for the course is designed to give applicants the opportunity to demonstrate their level of self-awareness. Questions are included about applicants' views on their current strengths and weaknesses in helping relationships, their reasons for choosing the course and their previous experience of working with other people. There is an open-ended final section which is intended to help in assessing the applicant's level of motivation.

The selection interview is conducted by two staff members, and lasts about an hour. In the tradition of the person-centred approach the interview is designed to create an opportunity for dialogue: the interviewers are concerned not only to assess the applicant's suitability for the course, but also to give the applicant an opportunity to form an accurate impression of what the course involves. The interviewers therefore aim to create conditions for a frank interchange, and to encourage the applicant to assess the course as much as vice versa.

The interview provides an opportunity to assess applicants' empathic capabilities. To what extent are they able to be sensitive to the interviewers in a situation which naturally encourages self-centredness? It also provides opportunities for assessing self-reflectiveness. In addition to these major themes the interviewers are also concerned to check on: (a) the applicant's capacity for theoretical study: this is seen as especially important since the course has no academic entry requirements; (b) the applicant's awareness of the effects which the training may have on his or her domestic life; (c) that the applicant can realistically afford the expense of the course; (d) that the applicant is primarily interested in counselling training rather than in personal development; (e) that the applicant genuinely wants to participate in this course, as against just any kind of counselling training.

*The M.Sc. course*

This is a three-year part-time course leading to a University of London M.Sc. in Counselling. Selection for the course has to take account of the University of London rules for entry to a Master's programme. Academic entry requirements are normally a first degree in social sciences or equivalent, but those without such a qualification may take an entry examination which has the form of a 7,500-word essay. The general aim is to encourage a critical and evaluative approach to counselling; applicants are preferred who do not already have much counselling experience.

The course is broad based. It does not emphasize any particular theoretical approach to counselling, and it is made clear at the interview that the psychodynamic approach in particular will not be prominent. The general framework of the course is constructed around the idea of the therapeutic alliance of counsellor and client, and this is linked with Egan's view that counsellors need different skills at different times within the counselling process.

Applicants fill in a standard application form, and all who satisfy the basic entry requirements are interviewed. Interviews last for three-quarters of an hour, and there will, when the second staff member is appointed, be two interviewers. In the interview the general points looked for are: (a) that applicants have made a firm decision to train in counselling as a career; (b) that they have some kind of experience of therapy or of settings in which they have experienced personal growth. This can, but need not, involve having been in formal therapy. Applicants are expected to be able to talk intelligently about their own growth. It is expected that applicants will be willing to have formal therapy during the course; (c) that applicants have some knowledge of the counselling literature; (d) that they can talk intelligently about their own strengths and weaknesses.

The interview is designed to be probing and has the secondary function of enabling some assessment to be made of how the applicant copes with a degree of pressure. An applicant is welcome to raise issues about what is happening in the interview; engagement with the interviewer is seen as important.

Two references are required; the second reference is taken up only in cases where there is doubt. References are not seen as a very important part of the selection process, since they tend to be uniformly good.

While there is not yet any set policy on age limits, it is likely that a minimum age of 25 will be preferred. No applicants to date have been over 60, but such applicants would be considered. Twelve places are offered per year to around 100 applicants.

*The psychosynthesis course*
This is a three-year part-time course leading to a Diploma of the Psychosynthesis and Education Trust. Prospective trainees first enrol in an introductory programme, 'The Essentials of Psychosynthesis', which is a representative sampling of what may be expected from the three-year course. This introductory programme involves fifteen three-hour sessions. It is taught by two trainers who complete an evaluation sheet on each student at the end of the course.

Upon completion of the introductory programme prospective trainees make a written application (in answer to a wide-ranging questionnaire) for a place on the three-year course. Each candidate then attends a selection interview with two trainers, who are not those involved in the evaluation at the end of the introductory course. However, the evaluation sheets from that course are used as part of the selection procedure. Thus four people are involved in the selection process. Selection criteria include previous professional training and experience, ability to form a helping relationship, openness to the transpersonal, capacity to deal effectively with the psychological and cognitive demands of the course, self-awareness, maturity and the ability to function co-operatively in a group with awareness and sensitivity.

Where there is disagreement between the selectors on the suitability of a candidate, ratings are made based on the above criteria. Each year 25 students are selected from about 75 applicants. Only about 10 per cent of applicants are simply rejected (with reasons being given to the applicant); others are often asked to reapply when they have fulfilled the selection criteria more adequately. Two references are asked for, but as with the other courses these are found to be of limited value because they almost always present a favourable impression of the candidate. There are no formal educational prerequisites for entry to the course. Students under about 28 or 29 years of age are discouraged, but not ruled out in exceptional cases. Most students are in the age range 30–60, several being in their late fifties or early sixties. There is no upper age limit.

**Assessment**

The assessment procedures in the four courses reflect not only their general philosophies, but also their detailed structures. In each case I will therefore begin with a brief account of the course structure.

*The WPF course*
The main emphasis of assessment in this course is connected with ongoing supervision of work with clients, special attention being paid to whether trainees are satisfactorily integrating theoretical psychodynamic notions both with their experience of clients and with their experience of their own development.

The course structure involves the following (there are some variations between the full, half and day-release versions of the course which I will not discuss in detail):

1  Seminars on counselling skills and styles, psychopathology, human development and other topics. Trainees' performance in these seminars is not formally evaluated, but seminar leaders may give feedback to the yearly Assessment Committee (see below).
2  Personal therapy: this is confidential and does not contribute to the trainee's assessment.
3  Experiential student group: this is a group of about nine trainees, which meets for 1½ hours each week. It is led by a staff member, and provides opportunities for informal and confidential peer and self-assessment. Such assessment is, however, specifically excluded from the formal assessment process.

4  Supervision group: this is a group of three or four trainees which meets with a supervisor for 1½ hours each week. The group is primarily case-oriented, but issues of group dynamics may also be explored.
5  Each trainee has a personal tutor, with whom they can meet to discuss general issues relating to the course.

At the end of the second term of each year each trainee writes a self-assessment, for which a standard form is provided. Trainees discuss the self-assessment with their supervisor, and on the basis of this the supervisor prepares a report on the trainee's progress. The trainee reads the report and may initial it to register agreement with it, or may wish to add comments if there is any disagreement. Each trainee also writes a case-study of between 3,000 and 6,000 words, which is graded on a pass/fail basis. Essays may be rewritten and resubmitted.

The formal assessment procedure takes place towards the end of each year, and involves an Assessment Committee which considers the progress of each trainee based on (a) the written self-assessment; (b) the supervisor's report; (c) the trainee's case-study; (d) feedback from seminar leaders; and (c) any comments from the trainee's tutor. Most of the members of the Assessment Committee will have had some contact with the trainee.

An external assessor from the Roehampton Institute sits in on some of the Assessment Committees, and gives feedback to supervisors and trainers. The external assessor also takes half of the scripts and evaluates the assessment procedure, making a report to the Roehampton Board of Examiners. In this way WPF has achieved an integration of external academic standards with their own norms of evaluation. The conclusions of the Assessment Committee determine whether trainees may proceed to the next year of the course, or, at the end of the final year, whether they receive their Diploma.

## The FDI course

The assessment procedure in the FDI course makes a radical break with traditional academic methods of assessment. The underlying rationale for the procedure is that, just as in the person-centred approach to counselling it is the client who primarily determines the aim and procedure of the therapeutic process, so in a person-centred training course it should primarily be the trainees who assess their own development and competence.

Throughout the course trainees are expected to assume a high level of responsibility for their learning. The function of the staff is seen as one of providing 'core' material and instruction, and resources upon which trainees can draw.

The structure of the course, which lasts 2½ years, involves six residential weeks, group supervision (in groups of about eight) averaging eight hours per month, and individual supervision/ personal therapy involving a minimum of 50 hours distributed evenly through the course. (No sharp division is envisaged between individual supervision and personal therapy, and there is no feedback from the individual supervision into the assessment procedure, except in the form of self-assessment.) It is also required that trainees should arrange for their own counselling placements, such that they can expect to see a minimum of three clients a week from the start of the course.

Five essays of about 5,000 words each are required, their themes being linked to the themes of the first five residential weeks. The sixth residential week is devoted specifically to the task of assessment; I will discuss this shortly. The residential weeks provide opportunities for intensive work in various groups: unstructured meetings of the whole course community ('the community group'), encounter and development groups (small groups in which 'profiling' takes place, whereby trainees explore their own strengths and weaknesses, and identify directions for future development), the supervision groups, and other groups for more specific learning tasks. The residential weeks also provide opportunities for counselling practice, role-play, use of audio and video recordings, as well as lectures, seminars, discussion and reading groups. Trainees are encouraged to contribute actively to the design and development of the training programme.

Throughout the course much informal self- and peer-assessment takes place through the group interactions. Trainees are expected to develop their own 'portfolio' of material which will reflect their development. This may include records of responses to set tasks, written self-assessments, and audio and video recordings of counselling sessions and role-plays. The development of, and reflection on, this material forms an important part of the self-evaluation work in the 'profiling groups'.

In addition to this continuous assessment throughout the course, trainees are required to produce before the last residential week a substantial written assessment statement. This is to include reference to the trainee's competence in counselling skills, their ability to conceptualize and describe their therapeutic work, areas of special competence, skills and attitudes which require further attention, and client groups with which the trainee is particularly effective or not adequately effective. In preparing this statement the trainee is required to consult their personal supervisor, at least two staff members, the profile group and the supervision group. The assessment statement is presented for the consideration of all course members in the last residential week, and trainees read and comment on each others' assessments throughout that week. It is planned to involve an external consultant in the assessment process in the future. The FDI Diploma is awarded on completion of the training, the trainee (with the assistance of staff and other trainees) thus making the final decision as to their theoretical and practical competence. At the end of the first FDI course one trainee decided that she was not yet ready to receive the Diploma, and postponed the award until she judged that she was adequately competent.

Staff assessment enters the FDI process in the following ways.

1  There is staff feedback on the essays written during the course.
2  If it appears that a trainee is reluctant to receive feedback, or in other ways does not seem to be participating in the self-assessment facilities of the course, a staff member will consult with them about what is going on, and reflect with them on the issues involved. Similarly, if a trainee appears to be encountering serious difficulties with any aspect of the course, a staff member will engage with them in connection with the anxiety the staff feel.
3  If staff misgivings persist it is an unwritten principle that the matter should be tackled no later than the end of the first year of the course. The matter will be fully discussed with the trainee, and some trainees do leave the course. There has as yet been no case where staff have judged that a trainee should discontinue, while the trainee has wished to proceed. If this did occur recourse would be made to an external consultant to help in reaching a decision.

The staff view is that on the first course the final assessment procedure worked extremely well. Trainees took the procedure very seriously, often going beyond what had been required in drawing up their self-assessment statements, and in the extent of their comments on each others' statements.

### The M.Sc. course

The course involves one full day and one evening a week, plus a counselling placement in the second and third years. In addition trainees are expected to engage in private study for at least ten hours per week. They provide their own arrangements for personal therapy, which is in no way linked with the assessment procedure. Supervision involves two hours per week at Goldsmiths' College and it is expected that there will be additional placement supervision. A range of theoretical courses are provided, a counselling skills group, an unstructured 'counselling forum' where trainees can raise issues pertaining to the course with the course tutor, and a personal development group. Trainees begin to see clients at the start of their second year. The broad-based approach of the course is matched by a broad-based approach to assessment, which is ongoing. In addition to the formal assessment procedures described below the trainees receive informal feedback and assessment from the course tutor, the skills group and supervisors throughout the course.

At the end of the first year:

1   Each trainee writes a self-assessment, in preparation for which journals are kept and discussions may take place with the course tutor.
2   Each trainee provides a tape of a counselling interview to demonstrate his or her counselling ability. These counselling tapes will be produced in the course of supervision, and will be reported on by the trainee's supervisor.
3   The skills-group tutor will report on each trainee.
4   There is an examination which focuses on aspects of counselling theory which are most important for seeing clients. All questions must be answered.
5   Two essays are required of 5,000 words each. Titles are suggested, but can be modified to suit trainees' own special interests.

The assessment at the end of the first year is designed partly to ensure as far as possible that trainees will be sufficiently competent to begin their placement work in the second year.

At the end of the second year there will again be a written self-assessment, a supervision report, a skills-group report and an examination. An essay of 7,500 words is required consisting of a review of the research literature in a special area.

At the end of the third year there will be the self-assessment, supervision report and an examination. In addition, trainees will undertake a piece of independent research on some aspect of counselling, or a dissertation of up to 15,000 words on a topic agreed with the course tutor. Finally, they will be required to write up an account of a psychological educational programme which they have run, for example, a day workshop.

All assessed work will be marked by the two course organizers, and samples of best/worst/average work will be sent to an external examiner. The M.Sc. degree is awarded on the basis of this assessed work.

*The psychosynthesis course*

The course programme involves one or two evenings a week, one weekend a month, plus a minimum of 24 individual therapy sessions per year. The monthly weekend programmes are devoted to a wide range of theoretical and experiential themes, which reflect the world-view of psychosynthesis. For instance, in addition to more standard courses on the history of psychology and theories of human nature, there are courses on Transpersonal Psychosynthesis in Daily Life, and Transpersonal Realization and Psychosynthesis Typology. The weekly sessions in the first year are for group psychotherapy; in the second and third year they are devoted to supervision in small groups. Group therapy is continued in the second and third years on a quarterly basis.

Each year a group of 25 trainees is enrolled, and they are assigned a Training Adviser, whose general function is to oversee each student's training, provide them with information and guidance and advise the Training Board of their progress. The Training Adviser meets several times a year with the group, and at least once a year with each trainee and another staff trainer to assess the trainee's progress. Trainees can consult their Training Adviser at any time, and conversely any concern the training staff may have with a student's progress will be communicated to the student through the Adviser.

Assessment is ongoing throughout the course; it involves self-, peer and staff assessment. Specific criteria of assessment are invoked, but it is an important aspect of the assessment procedure that 'the assessment process calls upon the intuitive perception of staff members, which will be utilized in all assessment procedures'.

*Staff and self-assessment*   At the end of each term the trainee's supervisor fills out a form on the trainee's progress, and the trainee fills out a similar form. The trainee reads the supervisor's form before it is filed. At the end of each year assessment forms are collected from all the trainers who have had contact with the student during the year, and the trainers' assessments are collated. The trainee then meets with his or her supervisor and another staff member. The trainee is invited to give a self-assessment for the year, and the trainers' evaluations are then discussed and compared with the trainee's self-assessment. In practice a large measure of agreement is usually experienced; where there are divergences both the content and the process of the disagreement are explored.

Self-assessment is also conducted through the maintenance of a training workbook in which trainees record and monitor their personal and professional development. This workbook (apart from the personal section) is brought to the yearly assessment interview.

During the course students also write four substantial papers. The paper at the end of the first year is autobiographical, and explores how the training experience to date relates to the trainee's biography. The second-year paper is a case-study of a practice client. In the third year there is a 4,000-word theoretical paper and a 5,000-word case history. The theoretical paper is read by the teacher of the relevant theoretical course, the case history by the trainee's supervisor and another staff member. Feedback is given by the staff on each paper.

Trainees are asked to request from their personal therapists some assessment of their development and competence, but the content of this assessment remains confidential to the trainee.

*Peer assessment*   This is informal. At the end of each year the trainees meet as a group and each trainee invites the others to share (a) what they especially appreciate about his or her skills and (b) what they feel this person would be served by developing. A staff member is present at this meeting, but the material is not recorded or filed. Peer assessment also takes place in an ongoing way through the working of the supervision groups.

At the end of the third year all the staff trainers meet. An external moderator observes and gives feedback on the meeting. Each student is discussed and assessed in the light of the agreed criteria, special emphasis being placed on counselling skills. The assessments made are recorded and this information is taken to the final assessment interview, which is conducted in the same way as in previous years. The Diploma is awarded on the basis of this final assessment, provided that the trainee has also fulfilled other requirements such as the completion of the required number of client-contact hours. A trainee who does not fulfil all the requirements may attend a further assessment interview when they are ready to do so.

**Conclusion**

It seems evident from this survey that there are important parallels between the different courses in their approaches to selection and assessment; there are also significant differences of emphasis. Among the parallels are: the concern to achieve a balance between assessing theoretical and experiential learning, the use of a range of assessment procedures involving forms of self-, peer and staff assessment, the discouragement of applicants under the age of about 28, the scepticism about the value of references, the sharp separation of personal therapy from the assessment procedures, and the concern to make the approach to assessment consistent with the general approach to counselling which is being employed.

The differences of emphasis are rather harder to characterize precisely, but they seem to reflect closely the philosophies lying behind the different approaches. In speaking of the person-centred approach of the FDI course, Brian Thorne emphasized the importance of power-sharing: that just as in the person-centred approach counsellors do not set themselves up as experts on their clients' problems, so counsellor trainers should see themselves essentially as 'resource persons' rather than as teachers. The emphasis in the course is very much on trainees taking responsibility for their own learning, and ultimately for assessing their own competence.

This attitude is also prominent in the psychosynthesis course, but there it is embedded in a further dimension of 'openness to the transpersonal'. Although the Psychosynthesis and Education Trust has moved increasingly towards the structuring and professionalization of its course, Diana Whitmore emphasized that the spirit of psychosynthesis, with its emphasis on intuition and the transpersonal, remains the ultimate determining factor for how the course is structured and run. She feels that the course has in fact benefited from the changes which were required in connection with BAC recognition, but the course staff were clear that had there been any serious incompatibility between 'professionalism' and the spirit informing their work, it would have been the spirit which had priority.

The M.Sc. course is the one which remains closest to traditional academic procedures; Windy Dryden remarked that examinations are a much-maligned form of assessment. This attitude goes against the tide of much contemporary thinking in the counselling world, but just for that reason it seems important to give it serious consideration. The academic world has its own values of commitment to truth, objectivity and disinterested concern, something of which comes through, I think, in the eclecticism of the M.Sc. course: of all the courses it is perhaps the one which involves least in the way of an initiation into a 'world-view' or a 'way of being'. (I say 'perhaps', because the values of academia themselves could be said to embody a world-view and a way of being. However a discussion of that would take us well beyond the limits of this chapter.)

The WPF course has a distinctive emphasis deriving from its roots in psychodynamic theory. One aspect of this is a greater emphasis on pathology than is found in the other courses. There is correspondingly a greater concern with pathological aspects of the trainee's personality and the potential these could have for harming clients. The intensive selection and assessment procedures reflect, I think, this profound concern or anxiety. The psychodynamic world-view could be said to be less optimistic (some would say more realistic) than those which inform psychosynthesis or the person-centred approach, and this quite properly has its implications for selection and assessment.

In conclusion I would like to link the four different approaches with the fundamental question of why selection and assessment are needed at all. The answer to the question, I believe, is that trainers have a professional responsibility to their trainees' clients, and that there is, therefore, an appropriate concern or anxiety that this responsibility should be discharged properly. What I suggest differentiates the approaches of the different courses to assessment is the kind of fear or concern which predominates. Iris Murdoch has remarked[3] that 'it is always a significant question to ask about any philosopher: what is he afraid of?', and the same applies to counselling philosophies. (A further aspect of this is the extent to which the fears and concerns of the originators of the different counselling approaches come through in the different approaches to assessment. I had a strong impression that something distinctive of Freud, Rogers and Assagioli lives on in the WPF, FDI and psychosynthesis courses respectively.)

In the case of the person-centred approach, what is most feared, I think, is abuse of power, and this is reflected in the emphasis placed in the FDI course on student self-responsibility and self-assessment. In the M.Sc. course I think the fear is that of bias, of drawing trainees into one particular mode of counselling, of initiating them into a closed cultish society where a disinterested point of view is impossible. Hence the maintenance of academic standards and values which have evolved precisely to guard against such dangers. In the psychosynthesis course I think the fear is that of a betrayal of the spirit, a sacrificing of intuitive perception and the spiritual to the requirements of 'professionalism'. Hence, although there is a formal structure of assessment, it is designed to give great scope in practice to the intuitive perceptions of the staff and trainees. Finally, in the WPF course, my guess is that the dominant fear is of unconscious pathology, the fear that apparently benign therapists may harbour pathological needs that will find expression in their work with clients: hence the very intensive selection and assessment process which works with unconscious as well as conscious aspects of the trainee's development.

## Notes

1 In March 1991 FDI changed its name to Person Centred Therapy (Britain).
2 Joel Kovel, *A Complete Guide to Therapy*, Penguin, Harmondsworth (1978), p. 79.
3 Iris Murdoch, *The Sovereignty of Good*, Routledge, London (1970), p. 72.

# 4  On Being a Trainer

## Brigid Proctor

**Introduction**

*On being me and being a trainer*
Being a trainer is a major aspect of being me. The context in which
I worked, and to which I was personally drawn, is quite untypical.
Throughout the 1970s and 1980s, I was influential in developing the
Diploma in Counselling Skills Course at South West London
College (formerly an Inner London Education Authority [ILEA]
College). Early in its life, this course was constituted as a self- and
peer-managed learning community, and later its student partici-
pants were delegated responsibility for self- and peer assessment.
Within this format, all the more usual training tasks found a place.
Additionally, in learning how to facilitate such a community my
colleagues and I had to address, perhaps ahead of time, some of the
tensions and opportunities which are likely to be at the heart of new
training initiatives in the 1990s.

Many of our principles and practices which seemed outrageous
to traditional educationalists and counsellors when I started as a
trainer are now commonplace. However, few trainers have experienced such practice at the receiving or giving end; and many find it
problematic, as we did, to integrate the reality of self- and peer-
managed learning within an overall concern for high standards of
counselling practice.

The invitation to write a chapter entitled 'On being a trainer'
gives me a very open brief. I have chosen to talk about my
experience at South West London College, since it charts two
decades of remarkable change both in the counselling training field,
and in my own personal and professional development. It also
accounts for some of my central preoccupations, which in turn have
influenced my training style and practice.

*A craft of the spoken word*
Since this is a personal account, I have chosen to talk in the rhythms
of speech rather than in a more formal written convention. Training
is an activity undertaken through the spoken word. For me, it is

also a highly physical activity – I almost always think about it in physical terms, and use physical metaphors to pass on my understanding. I come to it with heightened sensory awareness. Within a basic prepared course outline, I now most frequently act and then reflect, rather than think and then act. This tutored intuition is usually trustworthy. I would like what I write to convey that flavour. I want to echo my core preoccupation – how we, as 'people experts', can translate back what we have learned and reunderstood into language and practice which can enlighten and empower. All too often, I fear we deskill.

## On becoming a trainer

It is my observation that some people are born trainers, some acquire the training role and yet others have training thrust upon them. I am not a born trainer, nor even a counsellor by trade. I was trained as a social worker, on the first generic casework course offered in this country. I worked as a Probation Officer, becoming a supervisor to trainees. Three children on, I was delighted to take a lecturing post when we lived in the USA for three years. There I discovered that Introductory Sociology and Psychology, as taught to general studies students, offered simple riches accessible in a way which was not academic or rarefied. I wanted to make such ideas available to social work students when I returned to England. Part-time jobs in that field were hard to come by, and instead, I happened into a counselling course – at that time a 'scissors and paste job', with a little bit of everything and no formal counselling theory or practice – which was starting up at South West London College. So I became a counselling tutor without ever having been a counsellor. (In my defence, I would say that the psychodynamic casework I learned at the London School of Economics in 1955 was almost indistinguishable from the psychodynamic counselling now taught on some courses.)

There, mainly through the confrontation of some sophisticated students, I discovered new riches. Through them, and new colleagues, and through reading and working in new ways with my clients at Tooting Bec Day Hospital, the world of client-centred counselling, humanistic psychology and of systems theory opened up to me. It became clearer to me why the psychodynamic shoe with which I had been fitted in my own training, while elegant, fascinating and powerful, had never seemed quite practicable for my probation clients. I had often tried to fit their varied feet to the shoe, rather than really seeing their feet. With that clarity came freedom to stop the habit of judging myself and others according to the values implicitly embedded in that framework. Instead, I took on the alternative, and to me pleasurable, discipline of empathic understanding, communicated to client or student (or, indeed, myself) step-by-step. This was in contrast to my previous training of silent accumulation and clever interpretation. (I have continued to use psychodynamic *understanding* as a major theoretical underpinning to my work. With traditional psychodynamic *skills and practice* – both in counselling and in training – I continue to take issue.)

At the same time that I was immersing myself in new theory, I was also listening to the working situations of course participants. Many were already practitioners in widely varying fields, where they wished to develop counselling skills. At that stage, we knew little of what they needed in their work, and discussion groups were the major vehicle for finding ways to help them understand and practise.

*South West London College counselling courses*
Meanwhile, the counselling course at South West London College (SWLC) was developing too. After the death of Shiela Blain, the first ILEA Student Welfare Officer, who had initiated the course, I was left in charge of a baby I felt unqualified to rear. For me, it was a personal life challenge. For the first time, I realized that I would much rather play a 'critical-but-clever lieutenant' role, 'a friend to the students', than I would carry out-front responsibility. But I had bonded to the baby, and although it entailed making a full-time commitment that I did not yet wish to make, I took the post of Course Director.

To balance my lack of knowledge and experience, I engaged colleagues who knew how to counsel and how to train. I apprenticed myself to them – and what an apprenticeship. In the course of six years, I was exposed to a welter of ideas and practices brought over by successive tides of latter-day psychological missionaries from the States – client-centred counselling, Transactional Analysis (TA), gestalt, co-counselling, reality therapy, Egan's skills and developmental model, neo-behavioural counselling, bioenergetics – not to mention the more home-grown ideas of radical psychiatry, personal construct theory, social functioning and so on. I was driven to write/ edit a book (Proctor, 1978) to find some way of integrating what was good from all these; and to find out where they differed from each other and from my original training. (Cognitive models, and the amazing underpinning formulations of Neuro-linguistic Programming [NLP] came later and much later, respectively.)

## Self-managed learning community

In managing the course, we were naively perplexed by finding that whenever we altered its content and format in response to departing students' feedback, we failed to please the incoming students. We were also becoming uncomfortable about our differing styles, values and practices of training and counselling, so we called in a consultant, John Heron. Already pushed by the students to offer a second year and then a third year, we now found ourselves agreeing, at our consultant's suggestion, to develop the course as a learning community. Students would be facilitated to find what they needed to learn and then to negotiate with staff and each other to get their learning needs met. Because two of our staff members had direct experience of a similarly organized groupwork course, the idea seemed feasible, if daunting. At that stage, as far as I know, no one had offered an extended counselling course in this country based on these principles and practices.

It all seems a very long time ago now. What is of interest here is that up until now, I have found myself writing in the passive – 'I fell into', 'we found ourselves'; because at that time for me (not necessarily for my colleagues) that is what it felt like. I had no clear idea of where I, or the courses, were going. I seemed to follow my nose. Sometimes that would mean following some other person's nose, and sometimes it would mean changing allegiances. Soon we developed a shared set of values, ideas and practices which amounted to an ideology and a practice. With that came a growing sense of directing myself, and the immense satisfaction of joining with other self-directed colleagues and students to find ways to reach shared objectives.

The ideology was one of student-centred co-operative learning. Our ideas and values derived from Carl Rogers, from radical psychiatry and from the principles on which therapeutic communities were based. We believed that counselling students should experience in training the kind of empathy, genuineness and respect for their own personal directions which we wanted them to be offering clients. We also believed that this necessarily entailed becoming purposeful and confident in working with others. The learning community would be as resourceful or resourceless as they made it; their own intentional learning would be possible only to the extent that they experienced themselves as 'owning' the responsibility that truly lay with them.

## Staff role and practice

The practice involved the staff/trainers developing a 'student-centred', as opposed to 'course-centred', approach. We concentrated on recognizing and harnessing the resources which individual students brought. We supported them to reflect on their learning needs, within the overall remit of the development of counselling ability. This also entailed challenging them to unlearn some learning expectations (of themselves, their colleagues and their mentors) which originated in the traditional teacher-centred classroom. We encouraged them to find their own personal power, in the community of about 40 students and four staff which was the course, and to develop the peer support needed to do that. Only then could they negotiate with others to get their needs met. The staff role also involved reminding them of their obligations to support and challenge each other to work towards what they identified they wanted, individually and collectively.

*Means and ends*
At this stage, for me and I think for colleagues and often students, the means of learning became at least as absorbing as the ends. These ends were clear – to develop individuals' abilities to use counselling skills in their wide variety of roles and work settings. A lot of people learned that they could experience personal survival in a large group, and later, personal power. Most learned how to use the amazing wealth of experience, available in any group of adult learners, to supplement and enrich their own understanding and practice. They learned that to dare to be vulnerable was to find one's own resources, which had stayed sealed against the time when immature abilities and aspirations can dare to emerge into a safe and supportive-enough climate.

As trainers, we learned to devise and create, individually and collectively, structures, rituals and experiences which allowed these abilities and aspirations to surface. We coached and schooled ourselves and students on how to be respectful, genuine, accepting and understanding of what emerged (for our shared philosophy was based on Carl Rogers' story of the human experience). Few if any students thought counselling was 'only for clients'. They realized that the counselling climate and process was universally helpful in allowing people to gain confidence and self-direction, whether they were in the midst of learning, of changing, of misery, confusion, or oppression.

The initial role of the staff members was facilitating community meetings and groups. We reminded student participants of their various tasks, devised (or helped them devise) structures to help them accomplish those tasks. Only then, if staff resources were called on (which they mostly, but not always, were) we offered training, usually in the form of workshops or seminars. These might be on general or particular counselling methods; on psychological, social or political theories and issues; or on the development of interpersonal skill and awareness. Staff also led, or acted as consultants to, small ongoing groups where students worked to integrate their new ideas and practice within the existing frameworks of their life and work.

### The trainer challenged

This ideology and practice challenged designated tutors every bit as much as designated learners. Many of us were in the developmental stage that I have later come to identify, irreverently, as 'galloping growth'. It is typified by a self-absorption which can vary between the occasional and the absolute; by a capability for trust and engagement with fellow travellers; and by an intensity of hope and a capacity to tolerate pain in the cause of learning. I think such phrases as 'group transference' do not sufficiently convey the felt experience. Winnicott once said that every child deserves someone to be crazy about her (probably he said 'him'). Were this to be true of training enterprises, then the SWLC courses thrived, as their successors still seem to do, because there were a lot of participants in staff and student role who were crazy about them. They led us into fresh social and personal territory where we were all thrown on to our collective resources to make maps and find pathways. It was the mid-1970s.

### Getting a diploma

However, playschool and nursery school, alas, come to an end. Students who completed (I was going to say survived) three years felt robbed of external validation. A student and staff working party negotiated with the ILEA and the College Management to offer a College Diploma in Counselling Skills. It was agreed that the College would delegate to the student body the formal task of assessment.

A new role for staff emerged – facilitating students to assess self and peers. Students were now required to develop criteria and structures for assessment, appeals procedures and so on. We challenged them to maintain standards and be tough enough. We reminded them to guard against scapegoating likely victims and also to support those who, in role of assessor, gave good reason for judging others' evidence of skilful practice as being 'not good enough'.

And we also grappled with the informal task of sharing and differing about our own aims and standards as staff. We worked not to act those differences out through the students. On traditional courses, these differences of standards, of style and of criteria are grappled with (or sometimes avoided) by staff behind closed doors, leaving students to agree or disagree about the decisions. Here students had ultimate responsibility for criteria, standards and judgement. Staff could influence, openly or covertly, but we gave away systematic power. We fostered students' awareness that, once trained, responsibility for their own and their colleagues' practice would lie with them. The counselling profession is a peer community.

*Sugar in the diet*
I knew that, with formal assessment, there must come some loss of trust and innocence (or *naïveté*). Qualifications are like sugar in the food of an infant – sugar perverts the natural self-regulatory ability of young children to eat a balanced diet over time. Similarly, qualifications interfere with the self-regulating learning process. At the same time, I knew that we were no longer operating in some private corner of our own. We had developed confidence in our training and learning practice. Counselling was growing up and we needed to work with other trainers to see if we had some shared standards. We needed to be accessible to external judgement, through external assessors. We had responsibilities to consumers and clients with whom students worked. We were in the late 1970s.

Our first external assessors enjoyed our students' portfolios, but found them a little lacking in concrete evidence of applied counselling skill. We reported this back to the students who followed. Subsequent portfolios perhaps lost something in variety, but evidence of self-evaluated counselling work, and of the way in which each portfolio had been appraised by the student assessors, became standard.

*Accountability through supervision*
Throughout the life of the course, one forum for learning was non-negotiable. In those generous, subsidized days of the 1970s, students, within their small course fees, were obliged to undertake 32 hours of individual supervision in their final year. In those days, supervision could be by staff members, or by an approved external supervisor of the student's choice. In a course based so heavily on group learning methods, it was a one-to-one oasis for staff and student alike – the place where personal learning and 'out-there practice' at best could be married; or at worst be seen to be mismatched.

It also took care of staff needs to be as influential as we wished to be – it is tough to work on a course where your systematic power has been freely given away. Supervisors had no role in assessment.

A statement, agreed by supervisor and student, of strengths and weaknesses, was meant to form part of the portfolio of evidence presented for assessment. The supervisor contract stressed our responsibility, as supervisors, for openly addressing with the individual any reservations we might have about a supervisee's practice.

Subsequently, due to economic cuts, this heavy individual allowance was replaced by weekly group supervision (by a staff member) in the second year of the course, and 16 hours of individual supervision in the third. (This was one of the numerous examples of how we were able to relate creatively to changing external circumstances, and discover that necessity often leads to virtue.) As trainers, we were challenged to develop group supervision methods which accorded with the philosophy of the course. I think that most of us found these groups among the most creative and original work that we did (for an account of these group supervisions see Marken and Payne, 1987).

Supervision was non-negotiable because the aim of our counselling skills course, at its simplest, was to equip practitioners to use counselling interactions skilfully and appropriately in their working situations. Personal supervision was the opportunity for students to share working practice in detail. Here they could develop the ability to monitor their work. They experienced the intimacy of a one-to-one relationship, if they had not been in personal counselling themselves. And here they could receive direct personal feedback, and where appropriate, guidance and information from an experienced practitioner of their choice. In short, it was a safe and challenging forum in which to practise becoming accountable.

*You thought training was student contact?*
My work as a trainer began to be increasingly surrounded by other roles and tasks. I was responsible for devising a management policy and practice for staff which allowed for differences of time availability and pay. This agreement asked of us a similar discipline of self- and peer monitoring which we asked of students, while allowing for our different roles. As Course Director, I negotiated with the College and worked with other sections in the Management Department. I was taken in hand by more orderly colleagues and required to make some effort at an adult administrative style. As staff, each year we negotiated what personal responsibility each would take for a variety of tasks. These included setting up a rolling programme of residentials and staff development meetings; creating brochures and application forms; learning how to use audio and video equipment; creating a library and resource cabinet; relearning to use (and misuse) our secretary; devising self-selection evenings for students;

advertising and interviewing for tutors as we grew from four to a staff of 16; buying furniture and fittings; housekeeping; dealing with school keepers; negotiating our constantly moving course venues until we were finally given a home of our own for the last five years of my employed life.

As a staff management team we once covered a roll of lining paper which ran the length of the staff room with tasks and roles needed for the proper maintenance and development of the counselling courses. Every year, the Management Team (the full-time and almost full-time staff) negotiated the responsibilities each would take that year. With responsibility went autonomy to get on with the job, accountability to report on progress at an agreed weekly meeting and the promise (amply fulfilled) of support and challenge as needed.

With the new decade, I gratefully shed my Director role and handed over the task of Senior Tutor to my long-time colleague, Pat Milner, following our successful negotiation with the College that it could be a rotating post. By that time we consisted of four and four-fifths full-time staff, and two or three times that number of part-timers.

Concurrently, we were all bringing in and taking out ideas and practice. I visited centres in the United States which were developing the assessing of experiential learning; I chaired the Standards, Ethics and Accreditation Sub-Committee of the British Association for Counselling (BAC); I joined the Executive; I developed, with others from BAC, the Conference that grew into the Standing Conference for the Advancement of Training in Counselling and Interpersonal Skills – usually known as SCATS. All this seemed to colleagues (and I hope students) a necessary and natural extension of a trainer's task.

*And what about life?*
And of course, I was learning about remaining a wife; and being the mother of three teenagers in London. Looking back, it was one of the most rewarding and stressful times of my life. I was in love with my work and all it entailed. That left me sometimes feeling (and often being) absent for my husband and children. At the same time I was learning to be 'straighter' in my dealings with others. By the time my 'children' were moving away, I had finally developed a self-confidence in myself and my work that allowed me to make demands on my own behalf. Previously, I had continued a habit of being clandestine, learnt early in life. That led me to keep a lot of what I was engaged with to myself, juggling my commitments in a lonely fashion, which contrasted with my new-found delight in co-

operation at work. This in its turn gave rise to constant low-level anxiety which sometimes escalated into pain.

I needed then, as I need now when I am working, my own therapeutic 'maintenance space'. At one stage it was co-counselling; then biodynamic therapy. A steady period of TA therapy offered me some needed reparenting, which was followed by some mind-blowing NLP work. Each was chosen because I knew it was what I needed at the time. Each has contributed to my personal develop-ment, as well as being invaluable in widening my counselling and training skills. For the last five years I have had regular biodynamic massage – a maintenance opportunity which allows me to encounter old 'pits' and new panics with comparative equanimity.

About the time that I became a tutor, instead of a Director, my husband asked me an important question: 'All this talk of growth is fine, but what about the harvest?' He had a point. In addition to my training role and its extensions, I was keeping my hand in as counsellor and attending external workshops. I was a continuing apprentice both to my colleagues with developed training and counselling abilities, and to new full- or part-timers who joined us with skill and experience in different fields. I was also learning to accept the role of long-established colleague – acting, with other established tutors, as mentor to apprentice trainers on this rather strange course.

*Beyond ideology*
By this time (the mid- and late 1980s) I no longer had an ideology – I had developed, in its place, enough experience to know what was needed to help people achieve their learning objectives. I knew that nothing was totally predictable; and that many outcomes *were* relatively predictable. I knew quite a lot of short cuts in the process of group management of learning, and found myself inhibiting myself to the point of stress, lest my interventions either stopped people working out their own (and often fresh) solutions, or encouraged people to use energy reactively rather than proactively.

The world of counselling had become more established too, and there were some wheels that there was no point in inventing every time. My newer colleagues were into their versions of galloping growth (or of learning how *not* to make the same mistakes *we* made when they went on to develop their *own* courses). I more frequently offered the basic counselling skills workshops, in order to free newer trainers to extend their areas of experience. But I always invented at least one new workshop each year in response to students' needs, and this challenged and stimulated me.

*Harvest time*
And then I wasn't so in love with my work any more. For me, as a worker, I had for the first time in my life worked through a whole cycle – from start; to galloping growth and development; to young adulthood, maturity and establishment and I felt ready to move on. The time spent in student contact seemed to shrink, as the organizational pressures outside increased. I remain both child and adolescent, and although I enjoyed the sense of maturity, I wanted to be free of so much commitment, and hassle and change. The courses had produced a rich harvest, and for me personally, I wanted to enjoy the harvest that followed my galloping growth. So I took early retirement. (It was 1987, the College was due to become independent, and ILEA was in its death throes.)

As I reflect on what I have written, I am aware that students hardly appear in this account of being a trainer. That is not how it was. Somehow, through interaction between staff and students, within an increasingly clear contract, we created a culture for learning that had the strength and the pathology of its founding members (as I believe happens in all organizations). It was both reactive to traditional models and proactive for values which became clearer as we groped towards the objectives we set ourselves. It was a space big enough (we had anything from 25 to 70 course participants in each year group – most usually two groups of 40) to allow trainers from very different backgrounds, at very different stages of development, with widely varied personality, style and training, to work together. Of necessity, we had to talk, agree and contend together. Each tutor group would meet for half an hour weekly over lunch as well as meeting as a whole staff group for two days twice yearly at staff development weekends.

This, in turn, allowed us to relate to students from an amazingly wide range of age, background, culture, experience and education; to value – even be hungry – to discover what each brought to add to the pot available for learning. This richness was an integral and recognized part of the training experience. Student participants have written their experience elsewhere (*Self and Society*, 1984). This is my personal view and account of being a trainer.

*Life after South West London College*
I continue to train freelance, mostly supervisors, trainers or established workers. Passing on ideas, tips, exhortations in the role of external assessor, or consultant, has reminded me how much I have been privileged to experience; and what a lot I know about and have learned. Every year I do at least one basic counselling skills

course for some organization. It seems a big effort to force myself to go back to basics; to discipline myself, not always successfully, from taking the participants beyond their knowledge and understanding and deskilling them. But it is worth it to be reminded of the hunger that workers in the human services have for more creative ways of relating. It is still so new and amazing for people to listen to others, and really hear, and to be listened to and be heard. Mature learners are still surprised at being invited to create a working agreement with their tutors. To introduce people to, for instance, the Drama Triangle of TA is to see scales drop from their eyes. There is so much that now seems so obvious to me and my colleagues, which should be the birthright of us all. Yet it is totally unknown to trained teachers or experienced nurses, or busy residential social workers, let alone to their clients, patients and students.

So, in summary, my experience of developing as a trainer seemed to me to go hand in hand with the development of counselling training in this country. In the 1950s, I was trained in the new wave of psychodynamic casework training which was the newest and best to be had in the country at that time. Coming back to work in the 1970s after bringing up children, I met four new waves which had already affected counselling training profoundly, or were soon to do so. These were the humanity of Carl Rogers' person-centred counselling, the empowering insights of radical psychiatry, therapeutic community and group work, based on a mixture of systems theory and post-Freudian psychodynamic thinking, and the humanistic individual and group psychology and psychotherapy of Perls, Berne, Schutz, Satir and so on. Subsequently, in the 1980s, this heady mix was earthed for me, and many other trainers, by the quite comprehensive developmental skills model of Gerard Egan. By the time I met *The Skilled Helper* (Egan, 1990) I knew *what* I wanted for myself and others – Egan systematized *how* to communicate and achieve this. In the late 1980s, the elegantly formulated (but coldly worded) 'meta-models' of NLP have offered me a comprehensive enough framework to understand why *any* good practice may work, whatever theoretical clothes it wears.

The whole process of my development can easily be fitted into an Egan model – manic exploration in the 1970s; profound deeper understanding in the 1980s; and the whole transformed into a framework-for-action, just in time for the 1990s – the Age of Competencies.

**The harvest**

Being a trainer, my harvest has been rich. I have acquired an extensive network of contacts, colleagues and friends. Together, when we meet, we recreate an environment of support and challenge which leads to creative thinking, working and being.

I have developed abilities as a trainer. These spring partly from the acquisition of 'elaborated constructs'. They rest on developed personal and interpersonal awareness, and an integrated system of values. They are expressed through a wide range of ways of communicating – predominantly of speaking. This includes words, form, expressiveness and intentionality.

*The learning and training process*
In addition, I have begun to understand certain underlying dimensions of the learning and training process sufficiently to talk and write about them. In this way, I can continue to research and develop those themes along with trainer and student colleagues.

Perhaps the widest dimension is that of *the learning environment*. What is 'a good enough' learning environment? Carl Rogers told us about it. Winnicott has explored it. I now have new direct experience of it.

Within that dimension, I have come to understand and appreciate the need for *clear working agreements*. It now seems clear to me that agreed and understood work focus and work boundaries free people's attention for the task. I have experienced focus and boundaries that are imposed or assumed as being confusing and attention demanding.

I think I have often used the term 'experiential learning' without understanding or explaining what I mean by it. I now think I do understand it and want others to know what they mean by it.

Colleagues have introduced me to the idea of *archetypal roles* and I am fascinated by this. The possibilities and responsibilities of the training function, and the opportunity of sharing diverse roles with student members of a learning community, continue to delight me.

These dimensions – working agreements, experiential learning, archetypal roles – all converge in the *power dimension* of learning and training relationships. I now understand these as subtle and complex between learner and learner, between learner and trainer and between trainer and trainer.

In turn, all the previous dimensions feed into the dimension of *group experience*. Being a trainer for me is a continuing fascination with the personal and social energy which is generated when people group themselves together. I want to understand better how that energy can be channelled into power which furthers individual and collective energy. I have a need to recognize, respect and engage with power which arrests and protects against individual and collective development. As a trainer, I find myself continually working these themes in practice, in conversation and in my own head. They are the hidden dimensions of my experience. In writing about them, I continue to harvest them.

*The good-enough learning environment*
The working group – or shifting community – that developed at SWLC offered me the right degree of inner tension and outer stress – the right balance of warm support and honest challenge – for me to learn. It quickly became apparent that there was no way we could get things anywhere near perfect. If staff or students were deeply in the grip of what TA practitioners call the 'Be Perfect driver', this was no place for them. 'Be Good Enough', even 'Be Excellent' but. . . . We worked to support 40 differing individuals to relax and take their realistic freedom while doing their best learning. We encouraged them to be increasingly self-responsible while attaining standards approved of by some not very clear consensus. These aims were too complex for perfection. (Later we came to designate these strands formally as the Normative task – helping people develop standards and so on; the Formative task – helping them develop skill, ability and understanding; and the Restorative task – helping us all validate each other and develop a climate of sufficient safety and refreshment for creativity to flourish.)

The most to be hoped for was for us to learn to manage these tensions creatively, rather than destructively. We could then help students manage that tension too, in a way which enriched their ability to use counselling in their work setting. Nevertheless it was always clear there were plenty of things we (or I) could do better, and badly wanted to.

So there was present motivation. There was an intention of co-operative supportiveness, and a preparedness openly to appreciate others, which I had experienced nowhere before. There was modelling of widely varying practice and personal and professional abilities. There was generous sharing of ideas and information between staff and students. There was a shared agreement to stay as genuine as possible, which means challenging self and others. I do not think that any one of us could have imagined and intentionally built that enriched environment, but together we created a good-enough place for pleasant and painful learning to happen.

*Working agreements*
I came to understand that this learning environment was maximized when clear working agreements were made. For instance, students were increasingly offered answers to the questions, what am I

expected to learn?; what resources are available to me?; who is responsible for the different ingredients in this learning opportunity? what are our shared ground-rules and how flexible are the boundaries of time, behaviour, contribution, inclusion and so on?

The organizational agreement formed a structure within which we (staff, organization, students) were all, more or less, contained. Within that, we encouraged each Course Community to create their own contract with us and each other. In addition, each student made an individual learning agreement for themselves, with their colleagues. Those contracts, at best, were a transitional object for us all. They were holding-on rugs, or sucky rags, which were dependable enough as a reference point when times were difficult. They were proper protections to all in times of attack. Like a teddy bear, they could be loved, beaten, kicked and rubbished, retrieved, re-examined, reappreciated. They were our shared, social, objective agreements, which could still mean different things to all of us in our private, subjective, personal worlds. (This account of a transitional object is a quotation from Donald Winnicott, and is a symbolic understanding which I deeply appreciate.)

All such agreements (save the organizational one) would be useless as a legal contract in cases where shared interests do not 'take' – where some organic bonding does not happen. But they are invitations to all who agree (and this time I loosely quote from Gerard Egan, 1976) 'to act into your most trusting self, rather than out of your least trusting self'. To trust when you have insufficient information to know what you are buying into is crazy; not to trust from habit when the situation merits trust is sad and wasteful.

*Trainer as experiential learner*
Because of this background, I have disciplined myself to identify what I want to learn from any new training experience. I ask for help from a colleague (or if I am working single-handed, and it feels appropriate, from a course participant) to identify these learning wants. (This can usually be at the same time as the participants are helping each other identify their wants from the course.) In this way, I enrol myself as learner, as well as a trainer – and I can make intentional use of the potential resource that the course will uncover. It also helps me focus and separate out some strands of experience, for my own learning purposes, from the 'booming, buzzing confusion' which is multiple human interaction.

Learning done in this manner, I consider formal experiential learning. I am entering an intentionally structured occasion, with a formal learning intent. I suppose it is a bit different from the learning experience of the student. There the occasion has been devised and structured *particularly* to facilitate the learning identified in the course (or individual workshop) objectives. Such formal learning did happen for me when I was lucky enough to have the opportunity to join workshops devised by trainer colleagues or course participants, as an equal learner. It also happened on 'outside' courses, workshops, and in my own therapy (another formal experiential learning occasion.)

Both of these kinds of experiential learning I see as different from serendipitous (or informal) learning. Such learning is like the huge majority of learning I have (or, as I understand it, anyone has) ever done. We are offered (and give ourselves) an experience. We enter into it informed by our past and present knowledge, understanding and reactions. We have no clear questions in mind. We 'do' that experience our way – sometimes predictably, sometimes creatively, depending on the level of inner tension or freedom, and outer support or stress. If the experience has been good enough for us to bear to hold in awareness, we reflect on it according to our current favoured mental constructs; or we may invent or borrow a new construct to play with and draw conclusions from that. If it hasn't been good enough to bear to reflect upon, we may take care to avoid such situations in future. We may even plan our lives around avoiding them. Alternatively, we may seek similar bad experiences to prove things to ourselves about ourselves or others. We may come to think that is how life is – 'all learning has to come the hard way' and so on. These conclusions are then the basis with which we approach our next experience.

Significantly, for counsellors and trainers, we will pass on these conclusions to others, overtly or covertly. Being a trainer in such a complex environment has helped me drastically revise my assumptions about good climates for learning. I now want to challenge all new trainers, and counsellors, to identify how they believe creative learning happens. I now also hypothesize that, paradoxically, people cannot know what they are searching for until they are lucky enough to have experienced it in some degree; and that new and more satisfying climates can only be discovered as we, intentionally or unintentionally, risk breaking new ground.

*Trainer archetypes*
Understanding more about the mystical words 'experiential learning', and speculating on good-enough climates for learning, are possibly my central preoccupations. However, I am also fascinated by the rich opportunities that exist for trainers to develop unthought-of capabilities through role-taking. By this, I do not mean only the roles which go with the practical tasks which I have

mentioned, and the skill and qualities that 'doing' those require. It is also an opportunity to widen one's range of 'being'.

One of my colleagues asked me what archetypes went into taking the trainer role; we immediately identified a number. There are the Guru, or Wise Woman, from whom wisdom is expected, and the Earth Mother – the all-provider, unconditional positive regarder. In contrast there is the Clown or Jester – enjoying performance, and cloaking his truth in riddles, without taking responsibility for how it is received. The Patriarch creates order and unselfconsciously wields power. The Actor/Director allocates roles and tasks and holds the Drama; the Bureaucrat demands compliance to the letter of the law. The Whore gives services for money, which can be indistinguishable from love, and re-engages with group after group. There is even the Warrior – valiant for truth; and of course the Judge – upholding standards and impartially assessing. The Shepherd/Sheep-dog gently and firmly rounds up and pens; and, if there is such an archetype, the Communicator talks openly and straightforwardly about *what is*.

*Favoured roles*
As frequent, privileged and fascinated observer of many colleagues and teachers, I have encountered trainers who find it hard to extend beyond Earth Mother, and those who cling anxiously to Judge. I have been entranced and irritated by Jesters; expanded, seduced and bored by Wise Men and Women. I know people who cannot easily say goodbye to a group of trainees, who resent the Whore aspect; and those who stay in Patriarch and Bureaucrat for preference. I have admired Warriors, and then longed for them to lay aside their sword; and whereas one day, I may use the Communicator as a model, the next day, I may cover my ears against relentless communication.

*Hard and easy roles*
At the start I was wary of being too giving, and resisted Earth Mother role – these were self-managed adult learners after all and had to find their own way. My Jester feared being too serious – it was all a bit of an experiment, and I didn't want to be too identified with such a dark horse. It took participants to tell me that that attitude devalued the time, commitment and money they had expended; and that it also devalued the needs of their clients. My Warrior often operated with more noise than effect. However, I have always been a brilliant 'out-field' Sheep-dog – I value and enjoy the energy of 'strays' and am happy to allow them to find

their own timing and distance. Conversely, I can be too identified with them to be sufficiently dogged at penning time.

Later I could bear the Earth Mother role too easily, and found it hard to acknowledge the real power of the Patriarch, and the solemn standard setting of the Judge. I always found Whoring (strictly in the training sense, you understand) easy – each new intake of participants was absorbing to me. I came to appreciate that being a Bureaucrat – my most antithetical archetype – fulfilled marvellous boundary-keeping functions and gave energy for addressing the concrete and specific. I remain uneasy in role of Judge and Patriarch. The art of being an elegant Warrior still, I think, eludes me. I will always be grateful that happening into training gave many openings to my Actor/Director manqué.

**Issues of power**

*The Adult–Adult alliance*
Archetypes can be a useful way of thinking about being a trainer, because they raise the issue of use of power – another of my central preoccupations. Counselling courses are invariably offered to what, in the jargon, are called 'adult learners'. These people are established in their lives, occupy all sorts of roles, more or less successfully, have their established strategies for living, and they more or less 'know where they stand'. (It is probably a plus that they may choose to come on counselling courses when they are less sure about that than they have been, or others might be.) So at one level – the task level – as trainers we make a working alliance Adult to Adult – you want to learn; I have information, skill and understanding to offer.

*The Parent–Adult alliance*
What we offer is likely to be unsettling. It is, after all, about How The Experts Live, or suggest we Should Live. We can offer straight information about the myths of humanity as apprehended by Freud, or Jung, or Assagioli, or Rogers, and so on and so forth. Or we can offer more accurate ways of listening and communicating what has been heard. We can suggest people notice the messages they give themselves, out of awareness. Or we can challenge someone to say 'I' instead of 'one'. Any of these interactions can be quite invasive of an individual's established pattern of concepts and behaviour – of their personal and social culture. At the very least we are *inviting* them to see or do Life our way, and are proposing that they try out a set of cultural norms which may cut across many of their current cultural values. At most we are saying 'Only if you see or do it this

way can you be a counsellor – or at any rate get a certificate from me.' At this level – and especially where formal qualifications are at stake – we are in Parental role. We have power to give and withhold goodies, and people will respond to us in ways that they are accustomed to in dealing with Parental people – including previous teachers.

Even when, as on the SWLC courses, staff actively dissociated themselves from the formal assessment role (for better and worse), at some level students did not really believe it. We were still understood to be the people who had special skill, experience and understanding, and therefore would be the Judge. In the areas of how to use this learning experience, and how to use counselling skills in a work setting (the object of the course), we did indeed have special skills – so at this level we were in a Parent–Adult interaction. However, we presumed that trainees were their own *potential* experts on their personal ways of learning, their working situations, their particular needs as developing counselling practitioners, and most importantly, their own values and, ultimately, judgements.

### Invasion or deprivation?
At the same time, participants necessarily had limited vision of their rights and responsibilities as learners at the start of this (and other) courses, despite their prior agreement to the 'contract'. Some people knew from life experience what such an agreement entailed, but by far the majority were being invited into an experience which was mind-blowingly unfamiliar. And when people are in new uncharted territory, with a crowd of other more or less lost souls, they feel child-like, if not childish. At that level, staff were in a Parent–Child interaction. Whereas we were often worrying about the Scylla – Invasion of these adult learners – they were worrying about the Charybdis – Deprivation. What were we depriving them of that, if they had it, they could grow up and feel less depowered and deskilled?

### Parent–Child interaction
So as trainers we sometimes felt incredibly powerful – expanded, as it were, by the archetypal roles into which we were cast, and by the hopes, fears and expectations beamed on us by the collective community Child. We were lucky almost always to be working with other trainers, so that we could vary roles, and deliberately practise new ones. But of course we did fall into our accustomed, or dreaded, roles. And we did fall out with each other over it when the experience was too stressful to reflect on and handle. 'How come you take all the Good bits and I get landed with the Bad?' 'I

resent you being seen as the Expert and me as a kind of Hausfrau'. It seems an occupational hazard of being a Trainer to feel either too big or too little from time to time – grandiose or impotent.

I think my colleagues and I were good at remembering that, from time to time, someone on the course needed to hold most of the archetypal roles if good learning, expert practice and fair judgement were to happen. Our objective was to help students themselves distinguish what was in us and what was the projection each one personally enlarged us with. They could then have courage to take and play with these roles themselves in the service of their collective learning – to own their own power and creativity.

The rewards and relief came in watching communities become self-regulating, with the formerly powerless being heard and respected and the formerly powerful taking a rest. At such times, the Adult–Adult alliance was realized.

## The group

### *Group energy in the service of learning*
The learning environment, the evolving working agreements, the power alliances and the leadership roles are all social 'arrangements' fuelled by human energy (whatever that is!). This energy, as I simplistically picture it, is both the dynamic energy of, say, 45 individuals; and at the same time, it is the dynamic energy that is generated by their multi-level interaction. Interactions occur in pairs, in triads, in subgroups, within the organizational culture and subcultures – in total, they add up to the group energy. It has been my experience that when these social 'arrangements' are sufficiently intentional (that is, we all know well enough what we are about), consented to and owned (that is, we have taken enough time to negotiate and agree) and appropriate (they are suitable to our task, timing and resources), they serve predominantly to contain, focus and direct energy. Individuals have participated in understanding and creating them. They have a chance to include themselves and to check that others are including themselves. Such social arrangements both further the shared task and satisfy the social and psychological needs of individuals.

More often in learning situations these arrangements are insufficiently respectful of individuals and their proper social and psychological needs. They are laid down by those in authority, more or less clearly and openly. They are passively consented to individually (that is, by some individuals) and collectively (that is, by substantial unspeaking 'parts' of many individuals). In such situations, the group energy will leak, or grumble, or smoulder, flare and explode, in ways which arrest and protect against individual and collective development.

*Pro individual* and *pro group*

All this has been written about in many places, using a variety of imagery and often with emphasis on what is seen as pathological for individuals and for groups. As a trainer I have valued, perhaps more than anything else, the positive thinking and formulating of writers like William Schutz in *Joy*, an early 'Human Potential' classic, recently republished (Schutz, 1989); and of John Southgate, Rosemary Randall and Frances Tomlinson (1980); and of my colleagues Gaie Houston and Thom Osborn. These two led the way in modelling a practice which showed how group energy (which like physical energy is a neutral force) can be channelled through clear and open communication, into being not only pro the individual but also pro the group.

*Ages and stages, of groups and in groups*

To work with groups in this way, I learned that it was OK to like people and even to like to be liked – it creates a pool of nurture and goodwill to be dipped into in the tough times. It is an essential and sometimes undervalued quality in training. However, it is not OK to *have* to be liked. Whether or not it is an acknowledged part of the learning process, groups go through ages and stages, as do individuals during their life in an ongoing group. Being a good-enough trainer or facilitator includes developing a confidence to recognize and endure (or enjoy) healthy 'storming' and fighting. It is necessary to learn to distinguish this from destructive patterns of fight/flight, and the 'set-piece' battles of the Drama Triangle (the merry-go-round where people interchange between the roles of Victim, Rescuer and Persecutor.)

I knew this in theory long before I was able robustly to tolerate being The Baddie in practice. Later, I realized that some people learn best by finding and eliciting 'the bad' in their trainers. (In my experience they often go on to be successful using me as an anti-model Bad Object. Still later, I realized that that was what I myself had done with others, before I found Good Enough Objects to emulate.)

The point about 'storming' is not that it is, in itself, an end state, but rather, that without experiencing the testing of our potency in a reassuring-enough way, we cannot, in my understanding, go on to relax into our own individuality and autonomy. If enough course members break through that barrier, beyond lies the group experience where people can tolerate and enjoy a high degree of individual freedom and still work as a creative group. That is the reward for daring to be liked *and* hated as a facilitator.

However, I have also been through phases where I have gone along with a 'macho' training culture. At those times I feel wimpish if the students like me, and I can be unthinkingly provocative. It is very easy to forget the power and efficacy of 'counselling' responses in trainer role. Recently, working with an excellent, newish trainer I was able to intervene, with her permission, to prevent her blaming, explaining or justifying in reply to a covertly hostile question. On paraphrasing the question fully and handing it back to the course participant, the participant could make a clear statement of her complaint, and the feelings she was struggling with. As trainers, we could then acknowledge our part in the discomfort – we had offered a rather muddled set of instructions – and she could recognize her high anxiety when she was prevented from 'getting things right'. Acknowledging hostility, responding with intelligence and respect, and handing back what responsibility rightfully belongs with the learner can preclude a good deal of the most painful and destructive attack and counter-attack. And even doing that requires a good deal of courage for some of us.

*Structure and non-structure*
As I have moved from loose and wide to narrower and tighter in my objectives and expectations of students, I often meet others on

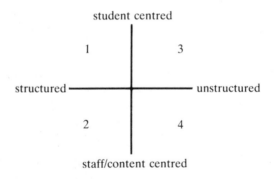

Figure 4.1   *The Structuring Matrix*

their journey in the other direction as they develop confidence. A matrix that one of my colleagues uses (Figure 4.1) may be useful for them. The figures are the order in which I have mostly spent my time.

1 A great deal of structured work helping trainees develop their own learning.
2 A lot of time in workshops – they are usually based on student-identified needs (except on short courses) but thereafter 'run' within quite tight structures with predetermined content and objectives.
3 Quite a lot of time (which often seemed interminable!) in community groups, with only basic structure, and with varying student- and staff-identified tasks.
4 Some time in workshops or large groups with staff-set agenda, but allowing trainees to find their own way towards that.

I learned that as I moved into less charted territory, it was useful to remember that 'student centred' need not mean unstructured; or that the staff have no place or personal power. The use of structures for learning – either simple pairs, triads and so on or complicated psychodramatic or sociodramatic 'productions' – may be more freeing for genuine student-centred learning (i.e. what students want to learn) than apparent non-structure.

Paradoxically, too, relative non-structure (for example, Bion groups) can be useful for staff-centred learning (that is, what *staff* want students to learn). More, it is legitimate, fun and instructive to play responsibly with any combination of the two, taking into account time-scale, participants and context.

### Biodegradable structures

What is beautiful about all the social arrangements I have been describing is that they are biodegradable. So many of the structures in which I have been reared – at home, at school, at play, at work – have been nonbiodegradable. I may have thought that they are well buried, but they have eaten into my mind, my body and my spirit. However I may disagree with the structure of the classroom, the family meal or the omnipotent boss, under stress I fall in and recreate it. 'Learn what I want you to learn'; 'Finish everything on your plate.' I may know I am right to challenge 'The Principal', but my stomach still turns as I knock on the door. Because this is how things are.

The South West London College courses developed drastic tactics to counteract and biodegrade old structures and social arrangements. In doing so, we learned that it is not possible to have 'no structure'; and that the anarchic state can confuse and oppress until people learn to manage themselves and each other by consent (as if the historians had not warned us!). So we borrowed, stole and invented an 'intermediate technology'. That meant structures and social arrangements invented, or borrowed, to suit *this* task, in *this* setting, with *these* objectives.

Tomorrow, next week, back home, we learned that we could readjust and renegotiate, change the rules, explore new roles, structures, contracts, power arrangements. At the same time we learned where we did not have power to do this. And we understood that sometimes this was because we were personally disabled, and sometimes because structurally we did not have power in 'the system'. Sometimes, even intelligent mustering of collective muscle was insufficient to influence things in the way we (or I, or they) wanted.

*What about counselling and counselling skills?*
I believe that this learning is integral to effective counselling. Not only does it help me recognize the 'social arrangements' suitable for my clients in the counselling relationship. It also, I hope, gives me sensitivity to hear and see what is their personal powerlessness, and what are the real social constraints with which they may be struggling.

In addition, the skills required – the flexibility of communication developed in these processes – cut across the cultural ways of communicating which embody uneven power relationships. I want to affirm my conviction that structured skills practice based on good modelling of true accurate empathy and the skills of positive challenge are *the* essential basis of any counselling training. I am also convinced that the content of the accurate empathy and challenge needs to be based on a personal experience of 'cross-communicating'.

**Conclusion**

In conclusion, being a trainer of counselling and of supervision has been infinitely rewarding. My major tool of training has been my counselling skill, and my intentional use of the counselling process – explore, understand, act – with groups and individuals. The ability to use these skills and that process with each other has been the major tool of students as they work together on the courses I lead or facilitate. I believe skilled counselling to be one of the most effective means of the healing and empowering of individuals. My experience as a trainer has extended my flexibility, my empathy, my genuineness and my respect as a counsellor, and as supervisor or consultant. As I have seen – and still see – generations of colleagues and students take those skills out into their work-places, affect systems powerfully or strengthen and heal individuals, I am moved by the cumulative power of well-directed personal and social energy.

## References

Egan, G. (1976) *Interpersonal Living*. Monterey, Calif.: Brooks/Cole.
Egan, G. (1990) *The Skilled Helper: A Systematic Approach to Effective Helping*, 4th edition. Pacific Grove, Calif.: Brooks/Cole.
Marken, M. and Payne, M. (eds) (1987) *Enabling and Ensuring: Supervision in Practice*. Leicester: National Youth Bureau.
Proctor, B. (1978) *Counselling Shop*. London: Burnett Books/Andre Deutsch.
Schutz, W.C. (1989) *Joy: 20 years Later*. Berkeley, Calif.: Ten Speed Press.
*Self and Society* (1984) Self-directed Learning: The South West London College Counselling Course. Whole issue.
Southgate, J., Randall, R. and Tomlinson, F. (1980) *Cooperative and Community Group Dynamics*. London: Barefoot Books.

# 5  On Being a Trainee

## Rose Battye

### Introduction

'Did you ever think I was a witch?'
It was about six months after I had finished my counselling training course and I was travelling up to London on the train with my children, in the holidays. Tom looked at me as if I were mad.
'Of course not.'
But Nell, who was eleven, was staring at me, very surprised.
'Yes, I did!'

She had forgotten all about it but the memories of many years ago came flooding back: the spindly cherry tree in the garden which concealed my den, the magic hour of 9.30 p.m. for making spells ('you *must* go to sleep now, it's 9.30'), the friends of mine who were also witches, and my magic powers (for example, knowing when she and her friends were talking at night even though they were making no noise at all). But there was a more serious side to it; I asked her if I had been dangerous. She said that I wasn't exactly dangerous but that I certainly wasn't safe. I remembered how I had been very concerned about her at this time. She had been physically very undemonstrative to me; she never hugged me or showed me any physical affection. If I kissed or hugged her she would receive it but make no gesture in response. I had thought I had just to accept that this was how she was, but it saddened and worried me. I asked her on the train if she had had to protect herself from me in this withholding way and she said that was exactly how it was. She couldn't respond to me lovingly in case she got drawn into my power. It hadn't ended suddenly; she gradually realized I wasn't a witch when she was about eight. But I didn't need to be told the date. I knew exactly when it had changed. My first and still most vivid memory of all the changes that happened to me during my counselling training was of coming home after the first residential week, walking through the front door, hearing Tom and Nell say something to me and realizing that I was properly hearing them for the first time in our lives, without any of my usual preoccupations, expectations or reactions distorting what they were saying. It was a dramatic moment which I shall never forget.

In the days following this incident I noticed that practically everything I said to them denied them and their feelings. It was horrifying to realize how I had never really allowed them to 'be' them; particularly as I had always prided myself on encouraging their individuality, and had brought them up believing that to be very important. Fortunately it was so horrifying that I had to start changing immediately. After only a few weeks Nell said to me one day 'You're so much nicer these days.' This time at the beginning of my counselling training fits exactly with the age at which she said she began to realize that I wasn't a witch. I can see now that being a witch explained to her as a young child the apparently impossible things I could do and know. But also, as I began to listen and accept and truly value her, the feeling she rightly had that I was exerting my will and power over her gradually dissolved.

I have used this story as my introduction because it describes the central and most important concept I learnt during the training course and one to which I return again and again in my continuing spiralling effort to learn and understand; the power of truly listening to and accepting another person. It is also an example of the enormous impact the course made on my life both in my relationships and in my understanding of myself. I learnt that damage can be repaired. Being a mother is no longer the battle it used to be for me; my relationship with Tom and Nell feels normal, healthy and equal. Nell is ordinarily affectionate to me now. This experience with them has given me great faith in the possibility of change on both sides. However, it was the first of many difficult truths I was to realize about myself.

It is just over a year since the course ended and in this chapter I am going to see what sense I can make of the last 3½ years. First, I am going to describe the structure of the course and say something of what happened within it, and then I shall describe what happened to me and how these changes were relevant to me in my process of becoming a counsellor.

### The structure of the FDI course in person-centred counselling

The course lasted for 2½ years, from September 1985 to April 1988. We had six residential weeks; one of these began the course, and then they were held every six months. In between we met for eight hours a month in small supervision groups, made up of eight or nine course members and one staff member. We could organize this time how we liked and in my group we agreed to meet one whole day every month. We each had a personal supervisor whom we saw approximately fortnightly. We were asked to prepare a piece of written work of about 5,000 words before each residential week, on a given title which was the theme of the week, and we had to find ourselves practical counselling work, initially seeing three clients and building up to about five clients a week.

At the end of the course we were asked to engage in a thorough process of self-assessment, with the help of the staff and other course members, and we were the final arbiters in deciding whether or not we received a diploma.

### The residential weeks

For me the most intense work was done during the six residential weeks. They were always held in some place far from my home which helped give me the feeling of being completely divorced from normal life. In general the weeks started with some structured work. For the first three days we were involved in practical sessions and workshops based on the theme for the week. I find it hard to separate this out as 'training' work because the material we used in our role-plays and groups would nearly always be drawn from our own experiences, feelings and thoughts. Our training in the core conditions was inseparable from the development of our self-awareness.

The more structured exercises were the starting points for our own experiential learning. I never felt that we had any limits on what we could draw from our own resources. Time, too, was no constraint. People would be late for, or even completely miss, community meetings or meals because they were involved in something going on in a small group. I had a real sense of freedom that I could use the weeks how I liked. I do not remember ever being told that I had to do or not do anything, apart from trying to fulfil the contract that I felt I had agreed to, when I accepted my place on the course.

In the second half of the weeks we planned our own 'community designed time', or CDT. I remember my initial feelings of irritation and panic when I saw the blank spaces in the timetable. No structure at all! But for me this became the most exciting time in the weeks. There was no shortage of ideas: many members of the group had special experiences and skills from which we could draw – for example, Aids counselling, or work with couples, or Jungian types. We could get together to work on subjects we wanted to go into in more detail – for example, some aspects of counselling theory, or the person-centred approach to dreams. We could spend more time practising skills to which we had been introduced during the week, using video and audio equipment; the staff would offer workshops such as psychodrama, or seminars comparing different therapeutic approaches. The days of CDT became absolutely packed, and the only problem for me was having to make impossible decisions as to what would have to be missed: would I go to 'death' or 'sexuality' or 'the child in us' or 'getting stuck'? Luckily, over the weeks, themes would re-emerge.

At least once a day we met together in the large community meeting. All the big issues of safety, trust, authority and power were raised by our experiences in this big group. I learnt a tremendous amount from what went on there; in fact, I believe that a large part of my 'training' in the foundations of the person-centred approach and my acquiring the attitudes of empathy, unconditional positive regard and, finally, congruence came about as a result of my experiences in the big group. It was here that I learnt how to be silent; how to be patient; how and why not to respond in an over-comforting, make-it-all-better way, when people are very distressed; how to listen, both by being listened to and by seeing other people listening and being heard. I experienced a wide and instructive range of empathic responses from the interactions; it was here I saw, experienced and understood the phenomena of projection, introjection, transference, countertransference and the rest. What is more, sharing in so much of other people's experiences, and seeing how they changed over the months and years, gave me first-hand experience and understanding of the therapeutic process.

**The supervision groups**

In between the residential weeks we met in our smaller supervision groups. It seems that they were all very different; I can only describe mine. Again we decided how we should use the time. Usually we spent the first hour or so catching up on how we all were and then we would agree an agenda for the day. Some people would want to talk about a client they were having difficulty with. Others had more general issues. Often people had a lot of distress in their personal lives; it was sometimes hard to balance the time we wanted to spend on work with the time people clearly needed to talk about personal matters. I was often amazed by how we managed to fit it all in. I had a love–hate relationship with these days. Compared to the freedom of the residential weeks they felt limited and res-trained; I used to feel the pressure of time, and on reflection I feel there was an inhibiting emphasis on unconditional positive regard and empathy (see p. 84). Nevertheless, despite these frustrations the supervision groups were welcome oases in my increasingly confused life outside the course where no one seemed to listen to each other and where I was becoming increasingly aware of feelings I hadn't known I possessed and that I didn't know what to do with. For this reason one of the most vital and valued structured areas of the course for me was the individual supervision sessions.

**Individual supervision**

It was in these sessions that I felt entirely sure of being safe and of being understood, accepted and heard. I would leave feeling clearer and calmer and more able to integrate everything I was experiencing and learning into my work and my life. Most of the time I would talk about clients and issues they raised. But the changes that were happening in me as a result of the course were so enormous that often these subjects would be related to some current confusion which I was experiencing.

My supervisor was comfortable with whatever I chose to bring. He always responded to me; it was 'my' time. I was aware, of course, that the time was to be used to discuss my work. His confidence and trust in letting me use the time in the way that would be most helpful for me was, I am sure, one of the major contributions to my learning to trust and accept myself. He was not at all passive; as time went on he became more challenging and questioning and more spontaneous about introducing his own thoughts, feelings and reactions; I could absolutely trust him to be fully 'himself' and yet in that precious hour he was there 'for' me. As I became more and more involved in the complications and confusions of my new life, this hour of clarity, in which I came to feel completely safe to say or explore anything, was vitally important and often the only time I felt I was receiving any affirmation about my 'new' self.

Supervision turned out to be a controversial part of the course, as I have found it to be generally in counselling training. Some supervisors felt they did not want to deal with personal issues apart from those immediately related to the training process or the work situation, and this variation caused distress for some course members. Some supervisors, too, were not themselves trained in the person-centred tradition, which resulted in further muddles. I know that great care has been taken on subsequent courses to avoid these particular sources of confusion.

There was one period where things became so complicated in my family life that I could see it would begin to dominate my supervision time and so I arranged to have extra time to deal with it with a different therapist. My own experience makes me sympathetic to the argument which says that personal therapy should be an obligatory part of a counselling training programme. This would have given us time to deal with the profound effects the course had on us and would have left supervision time (both individual and group) more clearly free for work issues. It would also have given us the valuable experience of seeing things from the longer-term client's point of view. It may be, however, that this 'best of all worlds' solution would prove prohibitively expensive.

## Work

It was a condition of coming on the course that we should be engaged in counselling work. I joined a doctor's practice on a council estate in Norwich. I was very apprehensive at seeing clients in the initial stages of my training, but decided I could do no great harm if I concentrated on trying properly to listen to people and to accept them while using my regular consultations with the doctor and my supervisor in a responsible way. I soon found myself in at the deep end; among my first clients was a girl who tried to commit suicide the week after our first session and a woman who'd seen the doctor about her depression and revealed to me in our third week a horrific history of sexual abuse. I was very lucky in that the doctor put no pressure on me to limit the number of times I saw people and, as a result, I felt absolutely free in the way I worked. The practice now employs me and is reimbursed by the Family Practitioner Committee.

## The course membership

Who were we all? At the beginning there were 36 of us: thirteen men, twenty-three women (I'm including the four staff members – one woman, three men). Over the 2½ years, a few people left. I was one of those who had no practical counselling experience but several people were established counsellors and between us we covered a wide range of experience and ability. Academically we ranged from those with doctorates to those who had left school at the O-level stage.

One of the first things someone said in the first community meeting was that we should never be strangers again. I had only thought of coming to learn about counselling; I hadn't imagined that the permutations of 36 relationships lay ahead of me and that some of my richest learning would be drawn from that complexity.

## Self-assessment

The sixth residential week was spent on our self-assessment. For this we had to prepare a long written statement of self-evaluation. A spare copy of this was available for other people to read and during the week we studied each others' statements and gave critical comments on them. To a certain extent the whole course had been a continuous process of assessment. For example, in the fourth week (on the theme of 'Therapeutic Process') our essay assignment had required the detailed analysis of work with a particular client. One of our small groups, the profile group, was used for monitoring our progress and for us to give our observations and responses on the changes we saw in each other at various stages of our training.

 · In the third week we did some counselling work with professional actors role-playing clients with whom we had great difficulty; we did this in groups of seven or eight people, with a staff member, who would all then give detailed feedback on our weaknesses and strengths.

When I was first told of the self-assessment aspect of the course, I couldn't understand how it would work. In the end I found it stimulating and rigorous. It made me thoroughly examine my attitudes and my work, and knowing that I had to share this process with all the people who knew me so well meant that I had to be as honest in it as I could possibly be. At the same time it was encouraging because I knew that admitting and knowing my weaknesses would be accepted and not be seen as a failure.

## The effect of the course on me

I want now to explore how I changed over the 2½ years and how the course enabled me to do so. These changes seem to me to be a vital aspect of the training for a person-centred counsellor, as without the development of self-awareness and self-acceptance, there cannot be a safe or strong foundation for the condition of congruence.* In fact, I would say that without a high degree of self-awareness and self-knowledge and a willingness to look openly at oneself, the use of congruence as an attitude can become damaging or even dangerous. For me I know that it is essential that I am able to observe and understand my own part in the relationship with a client so that I can be fully me, and properly be able to listen to her, without letting my own experiences and reactions get in her way. Before I was able to do this, I had to get to know myself thoroughly, understand my past experiences and all the aspects I'd been avoiding for years, as well as develop my self-awareness so I could know what I was feeling and why, at any time. Deep down, before the course, I had always felt a barrier of confusion between myself and everything and everyone else. I think I used to go through life impulsively reacting to everything, but not making very much sense of it all. The experiences on the course showed me how I could stop and consider what was happening inside me; and how to find out what I really thought and felt about things. This process began by making various discoveries about myself, most of which I had suspected but some of which were quite new. For example:

- I wanted everyone to like me;
- I found it very hard to give or receive anger and would do almost anything to avoid or deny it;
- I felt responsible for everyone and everything, and consequently guilty;
- I was very critical;
- I thought everyone knew better than me – I could not trust myself and needed constant reassurance;
- I thought I was evil and dangerous.

All these issues were raised through my relationships with people on the course and in the work we did together. Working them out took a long time for some were deeply embedded.

My fear of anger originated in my childhood where it had been a taboo emotion. I remember my mother being angry with me only once and it nearly frightened me to death. When I was a student, aged 20, this fear of anger was reinforced in an appalling and tragic way. For what seemed almost the first time in my life I was furiously angry with a very close friend. We had a row in the street. I turned away from him and stormed across the road. It was a dark, wet, winter's night and he followed me, I imagine blindly, and was knocked down by a motorcycle and killed. I left university, where I'd been studying philosophy and psychology, and went to live and work abroad for two years to try and escape from the horror of it all. Since then I had always felt I was a murderer and evil and dangerous. I had also taken great care never to be angry with anyone again.

When I came on the course and thought that I had entered a world where we could all be warmly accepting and dedicated to understanding each other and being nice to each other all the time, I was very happy. However, as time went on, I began to discover the limits of my own empathy and unconditional positive regard. To begin with I ignored my feelings of irritation or boredom. If someone said something that I disagreed with, or if I began to feel exasperated, I would try all the harder to understand their point of view and struggle to continue to feel accepting towards them.

Eventually my negative feelings became so strong that I could no longer avoid them. And so I was forced to become aware of feelings which in my normal life I had managed to disguise or deny. This process forced these feelings to the surface. At the beginning of the course I feel the conditions of unconditional positive regard and empathy were encouraged at the cost of congruence and I think this delayed our ability to be open and honest with each other. However, for my own process, I know that this suited me well because by trying to be all understanding and accepting, I was eventually forced to face up to other feelings which increasingly began to boil away inside me.

It was a difficult and frightening business beginning to tell people what I really felt but I learnt that instead of being destroyed, relationships are often strengthened by expressing these difficult feelings. Obviously the sooner they are shared the better; the danger for me is sitting on the feelings, out of fear or doubt, and then letting them out when they have become disproportionately strong. In the case of my university friend, he was the victim of years of my repressed anger. This kind of change has had a most profound effect on me as a person, but was also essential in my work as a counsellor. What kind of genuine relationship could I have had with a client if I had had to continue avoiding negative feelings both in them and in myself?

Another unhelpful attitude I discovered was my compulsion to feel responsible and therefore guilty about everything. I was an 'after thought' and had grown up with older parents who were also both ill. From an early age I had been in the position of being responsible and caring for them, and I received much praise and attention for being like this. The habit of feeling responsible was deeply ingrained in me but gradually loosened its hold as I began to see it manifesting in the way I related to people on the course. I began to see and trust people who were being responsible for themselves. I had to become responsible for myself, not for them. This also felt an important part of my 'training', as it would be most unhelpful for my clients if I were continually feeling responsible for them. I learnt the difference between being 'responsible for' and being 'responsible to' another human being. We were encouraged to be responsible for ourselves and for our own learning. At first it was very hard for me not to rely on being told what to do, but in the end it was deeply empowering to discover that if I wanted something I had to ask for it and that I could make it happen.

As time went by a few of my friendships on the course became increasingly close. The issues we tended to avoid in the big group, such as jealousy, competitiveness, anger and rejection, could not be avoided here. This intimacy feels a very important part of how the course changed me, as it has given me more confidence in knowing myself and being myself, as well as showing me the parts of myself I want to keep and the parts I want to let go of. One of these friends became very ill during the course and recently died. John meant so much to so many of us on the course that I couldn't write these recollections without mentioning him.

Another discovery for me was that there was such a thing as 'my stuff' and 'your stuff' (previously referred to as projection, transference, countertransference and so on). This was a complete revelation to me; I discovered that if someone was cross with me, it wasn't necessarily all my fault, and vice versa. Confrontation immediately became less frightening as I realized it could be understood and dismantled by trying to understand these ingredients within it. This understanding is obviously vital to my counselling work for it helps me see what may be happening between myself and a client as well as enabling me to clarify what may be happening in a client's relationships.

My feeling that I was dangerous and therefore evil stemmed, I am sure, from the accident with my friend. This was one of the last of my old attitudes to go. It meant that I could not really dare to look most deeply inside myself. I knew I should find demons there. I am sure it was the pervasive and powerfully accepting atmosphere of the course that eventually made me able to go into the dreaded place in a guided fantasy about our sub-personalities. Sure enough I had a room full of demons! It took a long time for me to open the door of the room where they were kept. There they were, huge and black, jeering with ghastly red mouths, waving their strong spiky tails about. In my imagination I banged the door shut. How on earth was I going to tell the rest of the people in the workshop that all I had as sub-personalities were demons? Eventually I opened the door and, as instructed, led them outside. To my astonishment, in the bright sunlight I saw them wilt before my eyes; their tails collapsed and they stood there, looking at me sheepishly. 'There's nothing to you, you frauds', I thought. 'You're all hot air and I've been scared of you all these years.' This was the visualization at the end of a long process, and it was after this that I really began to be able deeply to trust myself – not only my feelings and thoughts but also my way of being with other people.

These are the major changes that I went through over the 2½ years of the course. I didn't become someone who had total confidence in herself with no fear of confrontation, nor did I become totally aware and articulate without a care about what people thought. I still get in terrible muddles, am often full of

doubts, and speak and act before I think. However, on a good day
I think:

- I've become less impulsive and reactive;
- I am more able to understand things from other people's point of view;
- when I have the 'difficult' feelings, instead of avoiding or denying them, even though it is still sometimes very hard, I will try and face them, talk about them and see what can be done about them;
- I no longer have an inappropriate need for other people to like me;
- I no longer feel evil or dangerous;
- altogether I feel more able to trust and be myself.

I see my training as a beginning. I feel it gave me a solid foundation in my self-knowledge and in the acquisition of the fundamental attitudes of the person-centred approach. Sometimes I wonder whether I know anything. But recently I've been involved in training work and I've discovered that as far as the basic counselling 'skills' are concerned they are internalized and are now part of me. I know I am only at the beginning – sometimes I hear myself giving gratuitous advice; my attention wanders; I'm distracted by something coming up of relevance only to me. All this and more I take to supervision which I still have fortnightly. I am continually dissatisfied with my empathic responses and it feels like a lifetime's work to improve them. However, my learning so far feels thorough and I am sure this is because I learnt through my own experience and the course lasted long enough for me to be able to assimilate it.

I do not wish to give the impression that everything was perfect. Some aspects of the course were frustrating and unhelpful. I have already mentioned that the emphasis on the attitudes of acceptance and understanding inhibited our openness and confrontation with each other. This is my most serious criticism of the course. For too long many of us avoided our negative thoughts and feelings about each other. It was only in the last residential week that we freely discussed in the big group the difficult issues between us such as criticism, dislike, lack of trust and sexuality, as well as the jealousy, anger and competitiveness I have already referred to. We all regretted this and I know various changes have been made in the subsequent course, for example by introducing encounter groups into every residential week, to encourage greater openness.

Most of the difficulties I had to deal with during the course were as a result of the disruption it caused in my home life, some of which I shall briefly describe.

The contrast between how I behaved and talked to people on the course and how we were at home became increasingly marked. To begin with, as I became more aware of my feelings in general I could not stop talking about them. For a few months I had to stop going out socially with any one apart from those closest to me as I could only talk about 'real' things like death or sex, or what everyone was feeling in the 'here and now' or what I was feeling. Then as I began to express my negative feelings I seemed to be having rows with everyone all the time. It also took me a long time to stop responding in a counselling way when friends and relations talked to me about their problems. Even when I tried to be normal it felt artificial.

About two years into the course I became completely exhausted. I was finding everything – work, home and the course – impossibly difficult. The turning point came in a bizarre dream. In a beautiful landscape of rolling green hills and a pale blue sky I saw a huge red fish wobbling and heaving itself into the air; it was trying to fly and I heard the words 'it's a flounder'. (A flounder is, of course, a flat fish.) The dream made me laugh. I realized I was floundering and a fish out of water. After this I stopped trying so hard and gradually life became energizing instead of an exhausting struggle. It was a great relief to us all when I finally realized that not everyone had to share my way of being and I was able to control my levels of reactions.

## The little white card

There is so much I have left out, but to end with, I'd like to describe an unexpected event on one of the last days of the course. We were asked to complete a research project being carried out by a staff member on how the course might have changed us. At the beginning of the course we had had to sort cards with statements on them into piles on a scale ranging from 'strongly agree' to 'strongly disagree' and in the final week we were asked to repeat the process. One of the statements was 'I am a sad person'. I put it very firmly in the strongest *disagreement* pile. But when I looked to see if in this respect I had changed from my first sorting 2½ years before, I could not believe my eyes. Then, I had put it in the strongest *agreement* pile. I was absolutely dumbfounded – was I really so very sad then? I've often thought of how the course has changed my life, but this little white card made me realize just how enormous and deep that change has been.

---

* *Editors' Note*: In the person-centred tradition, for the counsellor to be congruent means to be in touch as fully as possible with the thoughts, feelings and intuitions

which make up his or her 'flow of experience' and to be able to give expression to these when appropriate. For the counsellor in training this level of genuineness or authenticity is often difficult to attain and the discrimination required to establish 'appropriateness' of expression even more demanding.

# PART 2   SUPERVISION

## 6   The Key Issue in the Supervision of Counsellors: The Supervisory Relationship[1]

## Robin Shohet and Joan Wilmot

> The process of supervision, like all human relationships, is fraught with hazards.
>
> (Rioch, 1980: 69)

> It seems that whatever approach or method is used, in the end it is the quality of the relationship between supervisor and trainee therapist (or counsellor) that determines whether supervision is effective or not . . . . There needs to be a degree of warmth, trust and genuineness and respect between them in order to create a safe enough environment for supervision to take place.
>
> (Hunt, 1986: 20)

In this chapter we will be focusing on the supervisory relationship. We have chosen to make this our 'key issue' because we have come to believe that when what happens in the room between supervisor and supervisee is openly negotiated, reviewed and available for comment by both parties, then the primary work of supervision – namely the bringing of clients – happens in a much more productive and fulfilling way.

When we first started supervising we would worry about such issues as our authority; whether we knew enough; writing reports; how or whether to confront if something did not feel right although we had no tangible evidence; how uncomfortable it felt supervising someone older, who may have had less counselling experience but more life experience; and so on. It is not that these issues have miraculously disappeared – just that we are more accepting of them. We now give ourselves permission to share our uncertainties with our supervisees when we consider it to be appropriate.

An additional reason for our focus on the supervisory relationship is that it is our experience that anything can be a key issue when the two parties are blocked or are blocking each other in some way, and nothing is when they are not. Thus, race, age, sex, ideology, boundaries, power, control, confidentiality could all be, and often are, issues. However as long as the two parties see it as their priority to explore the process of their working together, then the issues are in effect *vehicles* by which they can do this (and are therefore to be welcomed). Then the two people can see themselves as being on the same side, can drop their judgemental attitudes and be co-researchers in attending to the process in which they are involved which is being highlighted by an issue. So, in this chapter, rather than exploring some of the issues mentioned above, we will be focusing on what factors make for ease or difficulty in the relationship, and what steps can be taken to create a good working relationship, so that it becomes safe to bring issues.

**Fear and anxiety in supervision**

We would like to begin by examining the place of anxiety in the supervisory relationship. We are starting here because we believe that issues are often used as smoke-screens by both parties to hide fear of some sort. Here is an example from group supervision run by one of the writers (Robin) which illustrates this.

> At an alcohol treatment centre two workers are due to run a group together the next day. It is clear they are not prepared and there is considerable hostility between them. The obvious issue is that the black female worker has said repeatedly that she does not want to run the group and is only doing it because it is part of her job description. The white male worker is resentful and angry. They do not generally get on. There are all sorts of possible issues – gender, colour, the organization in which they work which has put them together on such a potentially disastrous project (setting them up?), personality issues. I share with the man that he must feel pretty helpless running a workshop with someone who says she does not want to be with him, and who would have no difficulty with a female worker; and that perhaps his response to impotence is to be angry, which I could understand. Perhaps he hasn't shared that he is in fact scared to be working in this way. He agrees he is anxious and hasn't shared this. She clearly has not seen this side of him, but has been caught up with her defensiveness. I guess, too, that she is vulnerable. She is a conscientious worker and knows she will not be giving her best. Yes she is anxious too – big groups make her anxious. I ask him if he knew that and he said no. They begin to realize they are both scared in different ways, and are defending. Then she pauses and says actually it's a group of white people – a large group of black people would not make her anxious. This is important for the race question has been brought up in a way that is not blaming. They are now on the same side.

Returning to one-to-one counselling supervision, being a supervisee and bringing clients to supervision can often be a very anxiety-producing business. It can feel, at times, as if one's whole identity is called into question. As one of our supervisees wrote, 'I felt very vulnerable, as if the supervisor's attention was scrutiny.' After one supervision session, again when there was no formal assessment involved, and when he realized that he had not handled a particular session with a client well, Robin wrote:

> I do not find being supervised easy. In fact after fifteen years I find it more difficult than when I first started. Then I was eager to learn, especially about what makes clients tick and more about myself. Now I think – there I go again. Does anything change? I imagine my supervisor being as critical of me as I am of myself.

In an article entitled 'The new supervisee views supervision', Cohen (1980: 78) writes:

> That the new supervisee will find the experience anxiety-provoking seems undeniable and unavoidable given the importance with which it is imbued at the early stages of a therapist's career. Some understanding of the bases for this anxiety will hopefully serve to reduce it to a level at which it can be used effectively to make supervision a rewarding experience.

While agreeing with this, we think it ignores at least half of the equation by missing out the supervisor's anxieties, and leaving the supervisee to carry anxiety for both parties. This is no more healthy than supervisees making out that all the problems are with the client, thereby denying their own difficulties. We often remember Bion saying 'In the consulting room there should be two frightened people.' This both validates the place of anxiety and makes it a function of what is happening *between* the two people.

In an excellent paper, Hawthorne (1975: 179) has described some of the inappropriate strategies used by supervisors to counter anxiety. She writes:

> Many supervisors, especially new ones, have difficulty adjusting to their new authority. . . . The balance which they have worked out for their personal lives between dominance and submission is upset by the new responsibility. The supervisory relationship is complex and intimate. . . . Sometimes the effort (to take on authority) is hampered by the supervisor's unfamiliarity with the requirements of his role, by difficulties stemming from personal experiences with authority, or by discomfort in the one-to-one relationship.

As supervisors generally have more experience, we think they need to set the climate for a tolerance of all the contradictory complexities inherent in a supervisory relationship. They can appreciate that it is not the anxiety itself that is destructive, but the denial, repression or rationalizing of it.

The causes of this anxiety can be numerous. Rioch (1980: 76) puts it quite simply:

> Unless the supervisor and the supervisee have a very unusual relationship or have already worked for a long time together the usual anxieties stirred up by strangers are likely to appear for both. 'How am I impressing this fellow?' is almost certain to be in both their minds.

For supervisees, in particular, the nature of the relationship they are entering might be unclear and this is bound to create anxiety. Even if they have had supervision before there are big differences in types and styles of supervision (see Hawkins and Shohet, 1989 – particularly Chapter 5). Whether new to supervision or not, the sort of issues that might be concerning them are described by Cohen (1980: 82):

> How accurately the student . . . will report what occurred in a session with a patient, will depend a great deal upon how the supervisor is seen. Is this someone who will accept my errors? Can I actually let on how I feel about a patient? Can I say what I feel about my supervisor? To what extent is the supervisor threatened by me? How much can I reveal and to what extent am I risking attack, both personal and professional, by doing so? While the answers to these questions may depend as much upon the student's maturity and world view as upon real characteristics of the supervisor, they are the data which the student will use in determining how deeply to participate in supervision.

### Previous relationships

Previous experiences of supervision and other relationships may colour how the supervisor is seen, particularly if such experiences have been negative:

> Trainees . . . are expected to expose themselves in supervision; to form a relationship with an authority figure who may be critical. This relationship is complicated by the likelihood of the trainee's transferring associations from other authority relationships, and therefore likely to invoke defenses which have characterized those relationships. (Greenburg, 1980: 88)

The transference feelings may be operating from supervisor to supervisee too. These feelings can lie under the surface unknown to both parties until an issue brings them into the open. For example, it may be only when a supervisee becomes angry with a new supervisor for not giving firmer guidelines that he or she realizes that there is unfinished business with a previous supervisor who let the relationship drift. The supervisee we quoted at the beginning of the chapter, who experienced the supervisor's attention as scrutiny, continued:

> My defensive reaction to this was anger and one week I was on the point of walking out. I actually started to gather my things together. The supervisor stopped me and I realized that I was checking to see if he could cope with my anger. I had a shock of recognition at this scene as it reminded me of how I test out other relationships.

As a practical suggestion for helping to deal with this, we often recommend that supervisor and supervisee share their history of giving and receiving supervision.

Because supervisor and supervisee may already be colleagues or may become so in the future, it is often not recognized that transference feelings can be as strong as in counselling itself.

## Managerial and assessment roles in supervision

Transference feelings can be especially prevalent when some kind of managerial or assessment roles are involved in supervision. This can cause both parties much anxiety, and bring up issues of authority for both. On top of this are the very real fears about needing to appear competent in front of someone in whose hands one's future may lie.

> Many of the conflicts in supervision reflect the fact that the supervisor functions both as mentor and as evaluator . . . . To the degree an evaluation is seen as potentially threatening, the supervisee is proportionately likely to be pushed toward performing for and pleasing the supervisor . . . . While the threat of negative evaluation may be functional in changing the supervisee's behavior, it may also create anxiety, further fostering less open interactions with the supervisor. While some anxiety is functional in providing motivation for change, too much anxiety may restrict the supervisee's openness and initiative. (Greenburg, 1980: 90)

The successful combining of what Greenburg calls the mentor and evaluator, we see as one of the main tasks in supervision.

The real or imaginary power discrepancy is an issue that needs to be addressed. To quote Rioch (1980: 71) again, 'The situation of "I am up; you are down" is stressful for both supervisor and supervisee. Furthermore it is ineffective. The supervisee does not learn anything.'

## Ability to handle conflict

So far we have looked at how anxiety, power, assessment and history can impede the supervisory relationship. Ability and willingness to handle conflict is also a very important factor in this relationship. Again each side will bring a history of this from other relationships. In an interesting paper, Moskowitz and Rupert (1983) cite many studies on the importance of the relationship. In one study they quote, none of the trainees openly confronted their supervisor and discussed the difficulties in their relationship. The most common method of coping was through spurious compliance. Trainees often closely monitored their communication and concealed pertinent information such as their personal feelings. Thus, when there are problems in the relationship, trainees seem to be more concerned with concealing difficulties in their performance than with exploring and learning from them. The inability of either or both parties to look at the relationship then becomes displaced on to issues. However, this was much less likely to happen when one of the parties initiated an open discussion about the relationship.

**Role modelling**

The acceptance of some of the supervisee's ambivalence, and so-called negative feelings, is not only important for the sense of safety and for ensuring that good (as opposed to compliant) work is done. It also acts as a role model for the relationship between supervisee (counsellor) and client. We tend to do as we are done to. Thus, if the supervisee has direct experience of an open discussion about the relationship moving that relationship on, they will be more able to initiate such a discussion with their clients.

**The supervisory relationship mirroring the counselling relationship**

The supervisory relationship and a willingness to look at it openly and consciously does not only act as a role model. It also opens up a technique of supervision called 'paralleling' (see also Chapter 10, pp. 160–1). By being able to comment on what is happening between supervisor and supervisee, there frequently dawns the realization that this is what is also happening between the supervisee and the client. For example, a very anxious client passes on their anxiety to the counsellor, who offers all sorts of useful advice, not because it is their usual style, but because they have unconsciously caught the client's anxiety. Feeling somewhat uneasy about what has happened, they bring the case to supervision, where the supervisor untypically comes up with lots of strategies for dealing with this kind of client. If a supervisor can recognize that they are behaving in a similar way to the counsellor, i.e. from a sense of anxiety and a need to sort things out, they can stop the process. Or if a supervisee can say how all this untypical advice is leaving them feeling, they too can stop this process and together supervisor and supervisee can look at how this situation is mirroring the one with their client. To do this there needs to be permission to comment on both what is happening in the relationship as well as what is happening in the room at the moment.

In another example a supervisee had a very withholding client who was brought to supervision, but in a very withholding way. The supervisor was able to feed back to the supervisee, 'I experience the way you are telling me about this client as quite withholding and I am beginning to feel angry. I wonder if that is how you felt with your client?'

To do this, which can sometimes be quite risky for both parties, there needs to be a good relationship. Our intention in looking at what we consider to be the main impediments to developing this relationship – namely, anxiety, power, history and conflict – is that by bringing them to awareness, they will be less likely to interfere. What we are unaware of, we cannot make conscious decisions about. However, awareness in itself is not enough. There has to be a forum, an agreed procedure whereby it is not only permitted to comment on the relationship by both parties, it is encouraged – so that we can deal not only with the *content* of the supervisory relationship (bringing clients), but the *process* of how it is done. In doing this we do not think it is possible or even advisable to remove all sources of conflict. They are the grist to the mill, and, as we have said above, serve as illustrative material for the supervisee in dealing with their clients. However, we think that there does need to be clear agreement between supervisor and supervisee about styles of working, and this will form part of the initial contracting.

## Clear contracting

The tone for supervision is set very early, mostly by the supervisor. Even with the best will in the world, every supervisor has biases towards which he or she will probably try to steer the supervisee. This is inevitable, but clear contracting can help to create a climate where as much as possible is explicit. In advocating an explicit contract to help make supervision productive and enjoyable, Hunt (1986: 21) writes about the need for a supervisory alliance which includes 'more openness and clarity on the methods to be used in supervision, and why they are used, the style of supervision, the goals of supervision, the kind of relationship it is hoped to achieve and the responsibilities of each partner in the supervisory relation-ship'.

As part of this alliance, ground-rules need to be established about frequency, duration, place and about how cases are to be brought, and also about how the supervision contract and the work will be reviewed and evaluated. We very much like the following statement by Brigid Proctor:

> If supervision is to become and remain a cooperative experience which allows for real, rather than token accountability, a clear – even tough – working agreement needs to be negotiated. The agreement needs to provide sufficient safety and clarity for the student or worker to know where she stands; and it needs sufficient teeth for the supervisor to feel free and responsible for making the challenges of assessments which belong to whatever role – managerial, consultative, or training – the context requires. (Proctor, 1988)

As with anything else it is essential to have goodwill. So a contracting session designed to sort out the supervisee so 'the bugger doesn't wriggle' is just another factor in some kind of control issue. Similarly, a supervisee who comes into the session armed with a list of requirements delivered almost as ultimatums is ostensibly engaged in contracting, but probably attempting to redress some kind of real or imaginary power discrepancy. It is worth mentioning, however, that supervisors do have, by the very nature of their position, more responsibility for setting the tone – perhaps by being willing to share some of themselves and not holding on to more authority than is necessary.

Even with goodwill, the complexity of the supervisory situation means that much will not be explicit. Greenburg (1980: 89) writes:

> Ideally, what happens in supervision would be mutually decided upon by both participants, on the basis of what is most useful for the supervisee. However, even if an accurate and mutually agreeable appraisal of a trainee's strengths and weaknesses were available, how to focus super-vision would still not be clear. This is because a supervisee's goals are complex and overlapping. What is available is also limited by the supervisor's biases and skills as well as the problems presented by one's clients. *So instead of a mutual decision, both supervisor and supervisee make independent, covert or unconscious decisions as to the focus of supervision.* (Italics ours)

We have on occasions noticed in ourselves and others the tendency for both parties to leave things vague so that when the going gets tough each can resort to their version of the contract, and feel misunderstood or even let down. At a day centre where one of us supervised, the manager allowed sloppy timekeeping by the staff, and when he wanted to assert himself brought up a person's lateness.

However, although clear contracting is essential, of itself it does not prevent issues arising, as the following example shows.

At the first session with a trainee counsellor, agreements were reached about length of session, frequency, what could be brought to supervision, regular times, style etc. At the second session Robin was about three minutes late by which time the supervisee had gone. Robin rang her that evening to ask where she had been and she said she had been there on time, and when he was not, she left. At the third session the supervisee wanted to know why he had been late, and Robin wanted to know why she had not waited. She said she was not going to hang around waiting as it was his responsibility to be punctual. He agreed, but thought there was more to it. She said 'let's forget it', but Robin said that he believed looking at the relationship was important. Had anything happened in the first session? Finally the student decided to share that she had felt angry that Robin had not been engaged – he had looked bored. He agreed that he was not fully engaged – that there was something which he did not understand about the way she presented, but thought in the initial stages he perhaps ought not to share that so quickly. The student then took a risk, feeling affirmed in her perception of Robin's partial non-engagement, and shared that she was on anti-depressants and did not want to be working. The process in the first session began to make sense and Robin could acknowledge that he might have been insensitive with his non-verbal behaviour. What had happened by an insistence on looking at the relationship was that both parties could begin to engage in supervision. There were no more power issues and in fact a very good relationship developed with the student writing openly about herself and tackling the supervision needs of her profession.

In this instance clear contracting and the supervisor's insistence on looking at the relationship were vital, but goodwill was also important. The supervisee could have elected not to share and the whole relationship could have broken down.

**Awareness of context**

As part of contracting, the supervisor needs to be aware of the context in which supervision takes place. Sometimes issues in supervision turn out to be issues about the context. Here is an example from a supervision by Joan.

Debbie was a deputy in a Children's Home. On the supervision course I was running she presented her supervision of Sue, a basic grade social worker. She was finding it difficult to supervise Sue who was defensive and resistant to supervision. We set up a role-play in which a member of the group played Sue and Debbie supervised her. However, despite input from the group, we did not make much headway, so we decided to ask Debbie about the context in which the work took place. It emerged that other workers at the home complained about Sue to Debbie, and were expecting her to deal with Sue in supervision. They were not, however, taking up their complaints with Sue directly. Sue was obviously picking up that Debbie had not only her own agenda, but other people's as well, so dealt with this by resistance. I asked if the team ever met as a team to look at how they worked together. They did not. I suggested that however difficult Sue might have been, the problem was not so much a supervisory issue, but how the relationship between Debbie and Sue had to carry unfinished business for the whole team.

In this example the supervisee became like an identified patient in a malfunctioning family, and it was important that the whole system was brought into focus, not just the supervisee. Organizationally it is hard to have open supervision in a culture where there is a great deal of mistrust and talking behind backs.

## The supervisor's roles and responsibilities

A supervisor generally has responsibilities to the supervisee, the agency and the client, and these can sometimes conflict. Skilful identification of these different responsibilities can often be crucial in promoting a good relationship. Here is an example of how looking at the supervisor's responsibilities in the original contract and the wider context helped resolve issues of boundaries and confidentiality, as well as an apparent personality clash between supervisor and supervisee.

Mary is a freelance supervisor who supervises John. He has applied for an internal job and been turned down. One of the panel who turned him down was Fred who is a friend of Mary, and also John's boss. Fred is also the person who has hired Mary as a freelance supervisor. John is annoyed at not getting the job and is convinced he should have got it. Mary knows why he has not because she has talked to her friend Fred, but can't divulge she even knows about John's failing to get the job before John brings it up himself. She feels a hypocrite, and in a dilemma because she agrees with the reasons. She also finds John generally difficult – unwilling to share anything of importance and look at himself. Further examination reveals that Mary's problems of confidentiality and her difficulties around John's reluctance to share (issues brought to supervision by Mary) are problems of boundaries and unclear contracting. She has not established to whom she is responsible; the agency as represented by Fred; or her supervisee, John. She decides to tell Fred that she refuses to discuss John at all and that she will make this clear to John in their next supervision. He is visibly relieved when she says, 'You know I see Fred socially and you must be wondering if we talk about you. I think I should have made it clear that I have told him that I am responsible to you, even though he has employed me and I will not talk about you or allow you to be discussed in my presence. Our contract is not managerial supervision as I am freelance, although if I think you are engaging in bad practice, I will confront you as I would any supervisee.' John is visibly relieved and begins to open up.

Here, looking at the wider system helped the supervision relationship, so that the apparent issues of confidentiality and withholding were seen to belong to the system and the contract. It was essential that the supervisor clarified to whom she was responsible. It can be useful for the supervisor, and perhaps the supervisee as well, to make a list of all the parties that have a stake in the supervision and to see if any interests conflict.

## Seeing many levels

The supervisor needs to be able to see many levels simultaneously, so that when issues arise they can be seen in a variety of ways. For example, a supervisee is angry with a supervisor for not being helpful enough. The easy and one-sided option for the supervisor would be to see this as the supervisee's problems with authority. If supervisors are more open to looking at themselves, they would perhaps look and see if they needed to hold on to power more than was necessary. However, supervisors would also need to be aware of the organization in which they work, and see how junior staff, for example, are left to sink or swim. The supervisor would also notice what is happening in the present, and would reflect on whether the supervisee is doing to the supervisor what the client is doing to them.

Without an ability to see all these levels a supervisor would take too personally a conflict which may not be personal, or have a one-sided picture of the issue. This could easily have happened in Debbie's supervision of Sue and Mary's of John in the above examples.

## Conclusion

In this chapter we have made the supervisory relationship, rather than particular issues, the central focus. In taking this approach we are saying that there are always issues in any relationship, and the ability and willingness to create the climate for processing within the relationship are all-important. This is put well by Krishnamurti (1976: 30):

> A disciple is one who learns all the time, and the word 'discipline' comes from the word 'disciple' – one who is learning. Now if you are learning all the time, there is no need to conform, there is no need to follow anyone. Therefore, the division ceases because the teacher and the disciple are learning. Both are moving in the same direction at the same time. Disorder means the lack of discipline, the lack of capacity to learn. When you are learning, there is no disorder. Disorder comes when you merely conform to what has been said or what will be . . . .

In other words the commitment to learning from both parties is crucial, and provides a certain kind of discipline. If the supervisor is not learning from the supervisee, as well as vice versa, then we have an imbalance which will probably manifest in some kind of power issue. The commitment to learning does not negate the necessity for clear contracting, or awareness of differing and perhaps conflicting responsibilities, styles and needs. Nor does it avoid conflict. It does mean, however, that there is permission to learn from whatever issues that arise, as opposed to avoiding them, or trying to cater for every possibility. This trust in process and relationship is not easy. However, our assumption, as well as our experience, is that given the right conditions people have a high commitment to learning, and the function of supervision is to endeavour to keep this channel open.

## Notes

The authors would like to thank Michael Carroll for his valuable help in formulating the idea for this chapter.
1 In many of the quotations we have kept the original words 'student', 'trainee', 'therapist'. They are equally applicable to trainee counsellor or counsellor.

## References

Cohen, L. (1980) 'The new supervisee views supervision', in A.K. Hess (ed.), *Psychotherapy Supervision: Theory, Research and Practice*. New York: Wiley.

Greenburg, L. (1980) 'Supervision from the perspective of the supervisee', in A.K. Hess (ed.), *Psychotherapy Supervision: Theory, Research and Practice*. New York: Wiley.

Hawkins, P. and Shohet, R. (1989) *Supervision in the Helping Professions*. Milton Keynes: Open University Press.

Hawthorne, L. (1975) 'Games supervisors play', *Social Work* (London), 20 May: 179–83.

Hunt, P. (1986) 'Supervision', *Marriage Guidance*, Spring: 15–22.

Krishnamurti, J. (1976) *Bulletin, Krishnamurti Foundation of America*, Autumn.

Moskowitz, S. and Rupert, A. (1983) 'Conflict resolution within the supervisory relationship', *Professional Psychology: Research and Practice*, 14 (5): 632–41.

Proctor, B. (1988) *Supervision. A Working Alliance* (videotape training manual). St Leonards-on-Sea, East Sussex: Alexia Publications.

Rioch, M. (1980) 'The dilemmas of supervision in dynamic psychotherapy' in A.K. Hess (ed.), *Psychotherapy Supervision: Theory, Research and Practice*. New York: Wiley.

# 7  Approaches to the Supervision of Counsellors

## Peter Hawkins and Robin Shohet

In his early days as a supervisor one of us (Peter) was supervising three different staff who were each in charge of a therapeutic community. He discovered that each person's supervision had a quality all of its own. One of them would bring his check-list of issues that he wanted discussed and decided upon. Another would engage him with a most interesting exploration of a problematic client within their community. Together they would explore the dynamics of this client and link it back to the understanding of this client's past and how this was being re-enacted in the community. The third would regularly start supervision by bursting into tears, and saying: 'It's all too much: I can't go on like this. Perhaps I am in the wrong job' – this despite the fact that she had done the work very successfully for 13 years!

Peter had allowed each supervisee to role-cast him in their own way. For the first he was a manager, for the second a casework tutor and for the third a reassuring counsellor. He sensed that somehow he was colluding with their own defensive patterns; and that to gain more from supervision, perhaps each supervisee needed him to play other roles than those they had seduced him into playing for them. However, he had no model or framework with which to make active choices about his own supervision style. It was this that motivated him to go in search of theoretical maps and for the two of us eventually to develop our own model.

We discovered that the approach taken to supervising counsellors will depend on at least five factors:

1  the style of supervision;
2  the stage of development of the supervisee;
3  the counselling orientation of both the supervisee and the supervisor (humanistic, psychodynamic, behavioural and so on);
4  the contract between supervisor and supervisee (does the supervisor have managerial or training responsibility in relation to the supervisee and their clients?);
5  the setting (individual, group, peer group and so on).

In this chapter we will explore each of these factors and how they affect each other, bearing in mind that they will overlap. However, we wish to stress that we do not see supervision as merely choosing from a menu of approaches. It is important to have a unifying concept that integrates one's own approach and makes the supervision more than the application of a technique or methodology.

Our own core concept derives from Donald Winnicott and we describe it at the beginning of our *Supervision in the Helping Professions* (Hawkins and Shohet, 1989: 3):

> The late Donald Winnicott, paediatrician and psychoanalyst, introduced the concept of the 'good-enough mother' – the mother who, when her child throws the food back at her, does not over-react to this event as a personal attack, or sink under feelings of inadequacy and guilt, but can hear this event as the child expressing their temporary inability to cope with the external world. Winnicott points out that it is very hard for any mother to be 'good-enough' unless she herself is also held and supported, either by the child's father, or other supportive adult. This provides the 'nursing triad', which means that the child can be held even when it needs to express his or her negativity or murderous rage.
>
> This concept provides a very useful analogy for supervision, where the 'good-enough' counsellor, psychotherapist or other helping professional, can survive the negative attacks of the client through the strength of being held within and by the supervisory relationship. We have often seen very competent workers reduced to severe doubts about themselves and their abilities to function in the work through absorbing disturbance from clients. The supervisor's role is not just to reassure the worker, but to allow the emotional disturbance to be felt within the safer setting of the supervisory relationship, where it can be survived, reflected upon and learnt from. Supervision thus provides a container that holds the helping relationship within the 'therapeutic triad'.

**The style of supervision**

In our own exploration and research on supervision we discovered that the main determinant of style was where the focus of supervision was centred. In 1985 we developed a process model of supervision, that both distinguished among the main different styles and provided a theoretical integration (Hawkins, 1985; revised in Hawkins and Shohet, 1989).

In this model we look at the range of options open to the supervisor, ranging from: exclusively looking at the client; looking at the counselling interventions with the client; the client–counsellor relationship; and focusing on the counsellor–supervisor relationship. Each is relevant at different times, but we have found that supervisors have their preferred areas of working, and by staying within their preference they limit the options for themselves and their supervisees. The options can be portrayed in a model as shown in Figure 7.1.

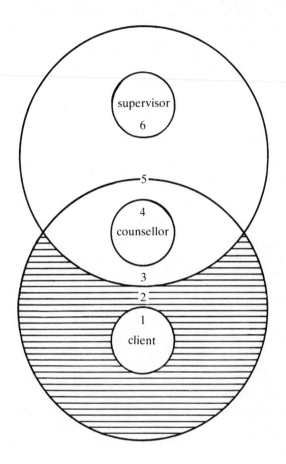

Note:  Shaded area is only available to the supervision matrix through some form of reflection.
The numbers in this figure refer to the numbered points that follow in the text.

Figure 7.1  *Six modes of supervision.*

## 1 Reflection on the content of the counselling session

Here, attention is concentrated on the actual phenomena of the counselling session: how the clients presented themselves, what they chose to share, which area of their life they wanted to explore and how a particular session's content might relate to content from previous sessions. The aim and goal of this form of supervision is to help the counsellor pay attention to the client, the choices the client is making and the relatedness of the various aspects of the client's life.

This is particularly useful when, through anxiety, a counsellor might label a client rather than actually 'seeing' him or her as a unique individual. Here the supervisor can use this approach to help the counsellor move back from judgements and towards paying attention to what 'is'.

> A supervisee presented someone who had been very difficult in a group and who had left early. The counsellor described the group member as 'a very angry woman who likes her own way'. The supervisor asked the counsellor really to focus on the opening few moments of the group in great detail, including how this particular woman had entered the room, where she sat, her physical posture and her opening remarks. It became apparent that she was giving signs of being insecure and the group leader (the supervisee) had not consciously picked these up.

## 2 Exploration of the strategies and interventions used by the counsellor

The focus here is on the choice of intervention made by the counsellor; not only what interventions were used but also when and why they were used. Alternative strategies and interventions might then be developed and their consequences anticipated. The main goal of this form of supervision would be to increase the counsellor's choices and skills in intervention. One of our colleagues whom we interviewed as part of our research described using this mode: 'I ask them what interventions they have made? What reasons they had for making them? Where their interventions were leading them? How they made their interventions and when? Then I ask what do you want to do with this client now?' (Interview with Helen Davies, 1987)

## 3 Exploration of the counselling process and relationship

Here the supervisor will pay particular attention to what was happening consciously and unconsciously in the counselling process; how the session started and finished; what happened around the edges (for example, beginning and ending); metaphors and images that emerged; and changes in voice and posture. The main goal of this form of supervision is for the counsellor to gain greater insight and understanding into the dynamics of the counselling relationship.

To start with, the supervisor might ask one or more of the following questions:

– What is the history of the relationship?

- How did you meet?
- How and why did this client choose you?
- What did you first notice about this client?
- Can you tell the story of the history of your relationship?

These questions must clearly be requesting something different from a case history and should help the supervisees to stand outside the counselling relationship in which they might be enmeshed or submerged and see the pattern and dynamic of the relationship.

Other techniques and questions that encourage this distancing and detachment are:

- Find an image or metaphor to represent the relationship.
- Imagine what sort of relationship you would have, if you and the client met in other circumstances, or if you were both cast away on a desert island.
- Become a fly on the wall in your last counselling session, what do you notice about the relationship?

These are all techniques to help supervisees to see the relationship as a whole rather than just stay with their own perspective. As well as encouraging a sense of detachment in the supervisee, the supervisor needs to have his or her own sense of the supervisee–client relationship which is impartial. In this way the supervisor acts like a couple counsellor, in so far as he or she must have the interests of both parties in balance. The supervisor should neither take the side of the supervisee nor the client against the other.

### 4 Focus on the counsellor's countertransference
Here the supervisor concentrates on what aspects of the counselling session and the client are still being carried by the counsellor, both consciously and unconsciously. A client, even though of a different age and gender, may remind a counsellor of their own parent, child or ex-partner, for example. This can produce rigid interventions, a lost and disturbed counsellor or inappropriate behaviour.

We also believe that clients can project on to the counsellor certain bits of themselves that they cannot yet integrate, and the counsellor for a variety of reasons will hold these either consciously or unconsciously. For example, a counsellor may unconsciously choose to carry a client's anger on their behalf, rather than risk eliciting the client's direct expression of their anger.

### 5 Focus on the here-and-now process as a mirror or parallel of the there-and-then process
Here the supervisor focuses on the relationship in the supervision session in order to explore how it might be unconsciously playing

out or paralleling the hidden dynamics of the counselling session (Mattinson, 1975; Searles, 1955). Thus, if the client were covertly acting in a passive-aggressive way to the counsellor, this might emerge in the supervision when the counsellor becomes unconsciously passive-aggressive to the supervisor as they discuss that particular client.

Here is an example from our colleague Joan Wilmot:

> I was supervising a social work student on placement to our therapeutic community who was counselling a resident with whom she was having difficulty. He was a man in his forties who had been in the rehabilitation programme in the house for about seven months and was now to move on to the next stage, which was finding himself some voluntary work. He was well able to do this but despite the student making many helpful and supportive suggestions, he 'yes buted' everything she said. In her supervision with me, despite her being a very able student, her response to all my interventions was 'yes but'. I took this issue to my supervisor, in order as I thought, to obtain some useful suggestions with which to help the student. However, despite the fact that I was usually very receptive to supervision, I responded to every suggestion my supervisor made with a 'yes but'. He then commented on how resistant I was sounding and how like the resident in question I was being. This insight immediately rang so true that we were both able to enjoy the unconscious paralleling I had been engaged in and I no longer needed to engage in a resistance game with my supervisor. I shared this with my student who no longer needed to resist me but was able to go back to her client and explore his need to resist. His issues around needing to feel his power by resisting could then be worked on separately from his finding voluntary work and he was able to arrange some voluntary work within the week. (Wilmot, 1985)

## 6 *Focus on the supervisor's countertransference*

Here the supervisor primarily pays attention to his or her own here-and-now experience in the supervision; what feelings, thoughts and images the shared counselling material stirs up in him or her. The supervisor uses these responses to provide reflective illumination for the counsellor. The unconscious material of the counselling session which has been unheard at the conscious level by the counsellor may emerge in the thoughts, feelings and images of the supervisor.

Robin Skynner in his latest book *Institutes and How To Survive Them* (Skynner, 1989) describes a similar approach used in family therapy:

> The therapist discloses his counter-transference response to the family and shares it with them not by attributing it to them but as a strange response in himself which he cannot understand. He thus provides a model of tolerance for a feeling which he thereby gives the family permission to own, if they are ready and willing to do so. The identified

patient often protects the family by picking up the family secret and running with it to the mental hospital. Some therapists protect themselves by lobbing the 'bomb' back into the family as an interpretation. With the group analytic approach the therapist, by defusing the bomb in front of the family, shows how it can be made safe or even that it may not be a bomb at all. (p. 106)

## An alternative model

A parallel model to the six-option process model described above has been developed by Hunt (1986) in her article on supervising marriage guidance (Relate) counsellors. She suggests that supervision styles can be divided into three types:

1  *case-centred approach*: where the counsellor and the supervisor have a discussion on the case 'out there': this is similar to our mode 1;
2  *counsellor-centred approach*: which focuses on the behaviour, feelings and processes of the counsellor: this is similar to our modes 2 and 4; and
3  *interactive approach*: this focuses both on the interaction in the counselling relationship and the interaction in the supervision: this is similar to our modes 3 and 5.

Hunt illustrates the dangers of using one of these approaches exclusively. If all the attention is on the client 'out there', there is a tendency to get into an intellectual discussion 'about' the client. There is also a danger of a large 'fudge-factor' – meaning that the supervisee hides material from the supervisor for fear of judgement.

If the approach is exclusively counsellor-centred it can be experienced by the supervisee as intrusive and bordering on counselling. Hunt writes: 'I am not sure how supportive this kind of supervision would feel. I guess quite a lot of learning would occur, but I suspect assessments might be made in terms of the trainee therapist's willingness to open up and talk about himself' (p. 17).

If the approach is exclusively interactive-centred, there are less dangers than in the other two approaches, but a great deal of important information could be ignored in the immersion of the attention in the complexities of the two interlocking relationships.

Thus, the trainee supervisor, having learnt to use skilfully each of the main processes, needs help in moving effectively and appropriately from one process to another. To do this, it is important to develop the supervisory skill of timing. It is also important to be aware of how different modes need to be dominant for different supervisees, and for the same supervisees at different times. This brings us on to considering a developmental perspective.

### The stage of development of the supervisee

Much has been written and many research projects have been carried out in the United States on the developmental approach. This approach suggests that supervisors need to have a range of styles and approaches which are modified as the counsellor gains in experience and enters different definable developmental stages.

We have integrated the developmental approaches from various American writers into a combined developmental model of four major stages of supervisee development (Hawkins and Shohet, 1989).

*Level I: The novice*
The first stage is characterized by trainee dependence on the supervisor. The supervisee can be anxious, insecure about the role and his or her own ability to fulfil it, lacking in insight, but also highly motivated.

New trainees have not had the experience to develop grounded criteria on which to assess their performance and consequently can feel very dependent on how their supervisor is assessing their work. This apprehension may be linked to the supervisor having some formal assessment role in their training or in their work evaluation, but will also be present on a more day-to-day basis in concern about how the supervisor is viewing their work, and how they compare to other supervisees with whom their supervisor works.

Level-I workers also tend 'to focus on specific aspects of the client's history, current situation, or personality assessment data to the exclusion of other relevant information. Grand conclusions may be based on rather discrete pieces of information' (Stoltenberg and Delworth, 1987: 56). It is difficult for workers in this stage to have an overview of the entire counselling process as they usually have only worked with clients in the early stages of counselling. This may make them impatient, or fearful that the process will never move on from a current stuckness.

In order to cope with the normal anxiety of level-I trainees, the supervisor needs to provide a clearly structured environment which includes positive feedback and encouragement to help the supervisee to move from making premature judgements of both the client and themselves to attending to what actually took place: 'Balancing support and uncertainty is the major challenge facing supervisors of beginning therapists' (Stoltenberg and Delworth, 1987: 64).

*Level II: The apprentice*
Here the supervisee has overcome his or her initial anxieties and

begins to fluctuate between dependence and autonomy; and between over-confidence and being overwhelmed.

In working with clients the level-II trainee begins to be less simplistic both about what is going on with the client and his or her own training: 'the trainee begins to realize, on an emotional level, that becoming a psychotherapist (*or other helping professional*) is a long and arduous process. The trainee discovers that skills and interventions effective in some situations are less than effective at other times' (Stoltenberg and Delworth, 1987: 64, italics added).

Loss of the early confidence and simplicity of approach may lead some trainees to become angry with their supervisor, whom they see as responsible for their disillusionment. The supervisor is then seen as 'an incompetent or inadequate figure who has failed to come through when he or she was so badly needed' (Loganbill et al., 1982: 19). Some writers have likened this stage of development to that of adolescence in normal human development, with level I being similar to childhood; level III early adulthood; and level IV being full maturity.

Certainly, level-II supervision can feel to the supervisor like parenting an adolescent. There is testing out of one's authority, a fluctuation in moods and a need to provide both space for the trainee to learn from his or her mistakes and a degree of holding and containment. In this stage the trainee can also become more reactive to his or her clients, who like the supervisor, may also be felt as the cause of his or her own turbulence.

The supervisor of level-II trainees needs to be less structured and didactic than with level-I trainees, but a good deal of emotional holding is necessary as trainees may oscillate between excitement and depressive feelings concerning not being able to cope, or perhaps be worried that they are in the wrong job.

*Level III: The journeyman*

'The level III trainee shows increased professional self-confidence, with only conditional dependency on the supervisor. He or she has greater insight and shows more stable motivation. Supervision becomes more collegial, with sharing and exemplification augmented by professional and personal confrontation' (Stoltenberg and Delworth, 1987: 20). The level-III trainee is also more able to adjust his or her approach to clients to meet the individual and particular needs of each client at that particular time. They are also more able to see the client in a wider context and have developed what we call 'helicopter skills'. These are the skills of being fully present with the client in the session, but being able simultaneously to have an overview, which involves seeing the present content and process in the context of:

1  the total process of the counselling relationship;
2  the client's personal history and life patterns;
3  the client's external life circumstances; and
4  the client's life stage, social context and ethnic background.

It is less possible to recognize what orientation the trainee has been schooled in, as by this stage he or she has incorporated the training into his or her own personality, rather than using it as a piece of learnt technique.

### Level IV: The master craftsman

This stage is referred to as 'level III integrated' by Stoltenberg and Delworth. By this time the practitioner has reached 'master' level – 'characterized by personal autonomy, insightful awareness, personal security, stable motivation and an awareness of the need to confront his or her own personal and professional problems' (Stoltenberg and Delworth, 1987: 20).

Often by this stage supervisees have also become supervisors themselves and this can greatly consolidate and deepen their own learning. Stoltenberg and Delworth (1987: 102) quote a colleague: 'When I'm supervising, I'm forced to be articulate and clear about connections across domains and that makes it easier for me to integrate.' Certainly, the stage of level IV is not about acquiring more knowledge, but allowing current knowledge to be deepened and integrated until it becomes wisdom.

In summary, the four stages can be seen as characterized by the central questions and concerns they address:

| Level I | – self-centred | – 'Can *I* make it in this work?' |
|---|---|---|
| Level II | – client-centred | – 'Can I help this *client* make it?' |
| Level III | – process-centred | – 'How are *we* relating together?' |
| Level IV | – process-in-context-centred | – 'How do processes inter-penetrate?' |

### Reviewing the developmental approach

The developmental model is a useful tool in helping supervisors more accurately assess the needs of their supervisees and to realize that part of the task of supervision is to help in the development of the supervisee, both within stages and between stages of development. The model also stresses that as the supervisee develops, so must the nature of the supervision.

However, there are limits to its usefulness that must be borne in mind. First, there is a danger of using the model too rigidly as a blueprint for prescribing how every supervisee at each stage should be treated, without enough reference to the particular needs of the supervisee, the style of the supervisor and the uniqueness of their relationship.

Secondly, Hess (1987) points out that supervisors are also passing through stages in their own development and we must therefore look at the interaction of both parties' developmental stages. This challenge is taken up in part by Stoltenberg and Delworth (1987: 152–67).

We now turn our attention to how the above two factors of focus and developmental stages relate to each other. As a general rule new supervisees need to start with most of the supervision focusing on the content of the work with the client and the detail of what happened in the session. New supervisees will also need help in seeing the detail of individual sessions within a larger context; how material from one session links to the counselling process over time; how it relates to the client's outside life and to their personal history. In helping the supervisee develop this overview, it is very important not to lose the uniqueness of the supervisee's relationship with their client, and for the supervisor not to give the impression that what is new, personal and often exciting for the supervisee can easily be put into a recognizable category.

As supervisees develop their ability to attend to what *is*, rather than being caught up in premature theorizing and overconcern with their own performance, then it is possible to spend more time profitably on the second focus of looking at their interventions. As stated above, here the danger is that the supervisor habitually tells the supervisee how he or she could have intervened better. We have found ourselves doing this when we say such things as 'What I would have said to this client is . . . . or 'I would have just kept quiet at that point in the session . . . .'

As the supervisee becomes more sophisticated then modes 3, 4, 5 and 6 (see pp. 102–4) become more central to the supervision. With a competent and experienced counsellor, who will have done much of his or her own conscious self-monitoring, the supervisor can listen out for the unconscious levels of both the supervisee and of the reported clients. The supervisor can then focus on the paralleling, transference and countertransference processes being played out within the supervision relationship.

## The impact of counselling orientation

There are some contexts in which the new supervisee will not require this progression of starting in the more content-centred modes, with a later progression into the 'here and now' process-centred modes (i.e. moving from modes 1 and 2 through to modes 5 and 6). A psychoanalytic trainee will need the supervisor to use process supervision from the very beginning and more behaviourally oriented counsellors may predominantly need supervision in the content-centred modes.

One's style as a supervisor is also affected by the style of one's own counselling work. If you are a person-centred counsellor it is most likely that your style of supervision will be non-directive and supervisee-centred. If your training has been psychoanalytic, as a supervisor you may tend to concentrate on understanding the unconscious processes of the client or the supervisee. If you are trained as a behavioural counsellor, then as a supervisor you will tend to concentrate on client behaviour and the methodology of the worker. In Chapter 6 of this volume it was suggested that bias in approach is to some extent inevitable, and can be usefully shared with the supervisee. It is also possible to integrate several different counselling approaches into one's own supervision style and this is explored by Boyd (1978).

Sometimes we are asked whether one should always ensure that a supervisor has the same type of training as the supervisee. There is no easy answer to this question, but both supervisor and supervisee need to share enough of a common language and belief system to be able to learn and work together. Sometimes having a supervisor with a very different training means that they are more able to see what your own belief system is editing out.

Supervisory style is also greatly affected by your own gender, age and cultural background, as well as personality. It is important to be aware of how these all affect the way you will view both the supervisee and the clients they will present to you. This is especially relevant when there is a match between the age, gender and background of the worker and the supervisor, but when the client has a different age, background or gender. For example, if the client is an elderly working-class, West Indian man, and the worker and supervisor are both young middle-class and white, the supervisor has to work doubly hard to help the supervisee explore how her own background and attitudes may be affecting how she sees and works with the client.

Eckstein (1969) offers a simple way of thinking about such issues, through considering our 'dumb spots', 'blind spots' and 'deaf spots'. Dumb spots are those where the supervisee or the supervisor are ignorant about what it is like to be in the position of the client. They lack the experience to understand what it means to be a homosexual, frightened of parental disapproval or a member of an oppressed ethnic group. Blind spots are where the supervisee's own personal patterns and processes get in the way of them seeing the client clearly. Deaf spots 'are those where the therapist not only cannot hear the client, but cannot hear the supervisor either. These are likely to involve particularly defensive reactions based on guilt, anxiety or otherwise unpleasant and disruptive feelings. Or hostility to authority figures may come into the picture' (Rowan, 1983: 161).

**Supervision contracts**

Brigid Proctor (1988) has shown how supervision combines several functions which she terms 'normative, formative and supportive'. This echoes the three functions that Kadushin (1976) terms managerial, educative and supportive. The presence and balance of these three functions will depend on the context in which the supervision is being carried out and how this is clarified within the supervision contract.

It is important for supervisor and supervisee to form a clear contract for every supervisory relationship, and in this contract to decide the managerial, educative and supportive responsibilities the supervisor is carrying. The first step in contracting is to be clear which of the main categories of supervision is being requested by the supervisee and being offered by the supervisor, and what sort of match or mismatch exists. The main distinct categories that we use (Hawkins and Shohet, 1989) are:

1 *Tutorial supervision*   In some settings the supervisor may have more of a tutor role, concentrating almost entirely on the educative function, helping a trainee on a course explore their work with clients, where someone in the trainee's work-place is providing the managerial and supportive supervisory functions. One of us (Robin) provided this on a counselling course where it was clear that his role was to assist students with their portfolio of work which involved writing up work with clients, but no managerial role was included.

2 *Training supervision*   Here the supervision also emphasizes the educative function and the supervisee will be in some form of training or apprenticeship role. They may be a student social worker on placement or a trainee psychotherapist working with training clients. This differs from tutorial supervision in that here the supervisor will have had responsibility for the work being done with the clients and therefore will carry a clear managerial or normative role.

3 *Managerial supervision*   We use this term where the supervisor

is also the line manager of the supervisee. As in training supervision the supervisor has some clear responsibility for the work being done with the clients, but they will be in a manager–subordinate relationship, rather than one of trainer–trainee.

4  *Consultancy supervision*   Here the supervisee keeps the responsibility for the work they do with their clients, but consults with their supervisor, who is neither their trainer or manager, on those issues they wish to explore. This form of supervision is for experienced and qualified practitioners.

**Supervision settings**

So far we have described only one-to-one supervision which is *vertical*, by which we mean it is a more experienced supervisor working with a less experienced supervisee. Vertical supervision can also take place in groups.

In Hawkins and Shohet (1989) we explored the advantages and disadvantages of supervising in a group setting. We saw the *advantages* of group supervision as:

– economical in terms of time and money;
– providing a supportive atmosphere of peers with whom one can identify and share anxieties;
– providing a greater range of input, reflections and feedback and consequently less domination by and dependency on the supervisor;
– providing a wider range of life experience, age range and so on, and potentially more of a class, race and gender mix: this makes it more likely that there are people who can empathize and even identify with both counsellor and client;
– providing more scope to use action techniques;
– providing an opportunity to learn from other people's successes and failures as well as one's own.

We saw the possible *disadvantages* of group supervision as:

– being less likely to mirror the dynamic of individual counselling as clearly as would individual supervision;
– you have to contend with group dynamics, which can be used as part of the supervision process (Rioch et al., 1976) but which can become either destructive or a preoccupation;
– providing less time for each person to receive supervision on their clients.

It is also possible to have *horizontal* supervision contracts, between supervisees of the same level who have formed themselves into a peer supervision group, and to have a one-to-one peer supervision contract. Peer-group supervision can be a useful adjunct to vertical supervision while a counsellor is in training, particularly in the later stages. It can provide most of the advantages of group supervision listed above while allowing the trainers to concentrate on providing individual supervision.

It is also a very appropriate mode of supervision for experienced counsellors (levels III and IV). This has become particularly relevant as more and more professional associations of counsellors and psychotherapists are requiring ongoing supervision throughout one's professional career – for example, the British Association for Counselling and the Association of Humanistic Psychology Practitioners. Many such organizations are also requiring that their members submit for reaccreditation at regular intervals, stating what supervision they are receiving.

## Conclusion

In this chapter we have summarized a number of approaches to supervision that have been developed in recent years. We have shown how these approaches are not contradictory but complement each other by attending to different dimensions of the supervisory process.

If we return to the three people that Peter was supervising 15 years ago, mentioned at the beginning of this chapter, we can in hindsight see that each of these models would have helped Peter be more aware of his choices when he supervised these three very different people. He would have realized at the outset that the supervision contract he was in with each supervisee was that of managerial supervision, and that he needed to balance the educative, supportive and managerial elements in his sessions rather than allow the supervisee to concentrate solely on one aspect.

Our own supervision model would have provided more options for switching the focus from the presented agenda, to working with the process as it emerged in the room and using what was happening in the supervisory relationship. In the case of the supervisee who regularly broke down into tears and altercast Peter as a rescuing counsellor, Peter could have used modes 5 and 6 to explore how the supervisee was using supervision in a way that paralleled how the clients used her in their counselling sessions. Then by moving back to modes 2 and 3 (strategies that could be used in the counselling relationship) there could have been a much deeper exploration of what was happening in her counselling sessions and how she might appropriately become less rescuing and over-receptive.

The developmental model would have helped Peter to recognize that the supervisee who brought the interesting case-studies was still very much at level II (the apprentice), with concerns about how effective he could be with the difficult clients he counselled. This could have been more directly focused on, rather than through a 'tutorial case-study'.

With the third supervisee, who brought his managerial check-list, there needed to be some exploration of style and differences in training. This counsellor had been trained as a forensic clinical psychologist abroad and brought up in a different culture. Both of these were probably key factors in how he presented for supervision and needed to be openly recognized and discussed.

If Peter had been able to provide for his supervisees a brief summary on supervision approaches, such as presented in this chapter, then there could have been an informed and open negotiation of the contract, style and focus of the supervision sessions.

Being clear about all these dimensions can lead to much better quality supervision. However, we would agree with Hunt (1986: 20) that 'it seems that whatever approach or method is used in the end it is the quality of the relationship between supervisor and supervisee that determines whether supervision is effective of not'. A quality relationship is not something that happens by chance, but is built over time by both the supervisor and supervisee actively attending both to their joint task and how they are working and relating together.

## References

Boyd, J. (1978) *Counselor Supervision: Approaches, Preparation, Practices*. Muncie, Indiana: Accelerated Development.

Eckstein, R. (1969) 'Concerning the teaching and learning of psychoanalysis', *Journal of the American Psychoanalytic Association*, 17 (2): 312–32.

Hawkins, P. (1985) 'Humanistic psychotherapy supervision: a conceptual framework', *Self and Society: European Journal of Humanistic Psychology*, 13 (2): 69–77.

Hawkins, P. and Shohet, R. (1989) *Supervision in the Helping Professions*. Milton Keynes: Open University Press.

Hess, A.K. (1987) 'Psychotherapy supervision: stages, Buber and a theory of relationship', *Professional Psychology: Research and Practice*, 18 (3): 251–9.

Hunt, P. (1986) 'Supervision', *Marriage Guidance*, Spring: 15–22.

Kadushin, A. (1976) *Supervision in Social Work*. New York: Columbia University Press.

Loganbill, C., Hardy, E., and Delworth, U. (1982) 'Supervision, a conceptual model', *Counseling Psychologist*, 10 (1): 3–42.
Mattinson, J. (1975) *The Reflection Process in Casework Supervision*. London: Institute of Marital Studies.
Proctor, B. (1988) *Supervision: A Working Alliance* (videotape training manual). St Leonards-on-Sea, East Sussex: Alexia Publications.
Rioch, M.J., Coulter, W.R. and Weinberger, D.M. (1976) *Dialogues for Therapists*. San Francisco: Jossey-Bass.
Rowan, J. (1983) *Reality Game: A Guide to Humanistic Counselling and Therapy*. London: Routledge & Kegan Paul.
Searles, H.F. (1955) 'The information value of the supervisor's emotional experience', in *Collected Papers of Schizophrenia and Related Subjects*. London: Hogarth Press.
Skynner R. (1989) *Institutes and How to Survive Them*. London: Methuen.
Stoltenberg, C.D. and Delworth, U. (1987) *Supervising Counselors and Therapists*. San Francisco: Jossey-Bass.
Wilmot, J. (1985) 'Paralleling in the supervision process', *Self and Society: European Journal of Humanistic Psychology*, 13 (2): 86–92.

# 8 On Being a Supervisor

## Dave Mearns

In this chapter I shall concentrate on my experience of individual supervision with professional counsellors, though some illustrations will be drawn from events in group supervision with trainee counsellors and psychotherapists. Whatever the supervision context, however, experience has shown me that my most important task is to establish the kind of relationship which makes possible the freedom and non-defensiveness desired, for example, by a social work supervisee who in her second session with me made it quite clear what she wanted from supervision:

> After our last session I felt really annoyed with myself. I had wanted to use you as one person with whom I could really open out, but I ended up not saying how bad it all was for me and how inadequate I felt. I did the same thing with you as I do with my Senior [her social work supervisor] – I presented a picture of 'work is bloody hard, but I can cope'. Whereas what I really feel is that I *can't* cope – I'm falling apart – sometimes I am getting the shakes so bad that I have to wait in the car before going in to see a family. Sometimes I dodge jobs because I can't cope. One time I drove into the country to find a place to cry. I have come to you because there's no way I can take that stuff to my supervisor. I can't really fall apart with him – I've got to maintain the same pretence which we all do.[1]

This social worker was not in need of therapy even though her stress sounds severe. That stress had become intensified partly because of the lack of adequate supervision in her social work context in which she could talk freely and fully about her emotional experiencing in relation to the work. The kind of supervision relationship which I wish to provide offers the independence and support necessary for the supervisee to feel a freedom which is not evident in other contexts. It is for this reason that I find as much demand for counselling supervision coming from social workers, medical and care workers, and individuals in senior and middle management, as I do from counsellors. All these professionals value a relationship where they are free to explore work-related concerns which they believe could not be divulged to anyone in their own organization.

**Establishing a healthy supervision relationship**

In seeking to create a relationship which will foster the supervisee's professional growth, I need to be the kind of person with whom she can feel safe enough to express even her deepest fears and doubts. For me, this involves establishing a relationship where I am challenged to offer four basic 'conditions'. The first is my *commitment* to the supervisee. 'Commitment' is not simply the reliability afforded by regular meetings; it is an undertaking that I will be fully involved in our relationship – that I, for my part, will be prepared to fight for the health of our relationship no matter what difficulties we may encounter. Any relationship can develop norms which restrict the functioning of the individuals involved – it is easy to slip into superficial ways of relating which avoid both challenge and close meeting. 'Commitment' to the relationship is an aspect of professionalism which forces me as the supervisor to address difficulties in the relationship even though my inclination may be to run away from them.

A related condition is my *congruence* as a supervisor. This is a technical term referring to the degree to which I am able and willing to be transparent in relation to the counsellor. Congruence releases my perceptions, insights and reactions to the supervisee in such a way that our relationship can be used therapeutically. Although it is a supervision rather than a therapy relationship, the same therapeutic principles apply with regard to the facilitation of insight and the development of trust. A full exploration of congruence, as indeed of the other conditions discussed here, can be found in Mearns and Thorne (1988).

The third condition which determines the health of the supervision relationship is the nature of my *valuing* of the supervisee. If this valuing is at all partial or conditional then the material which the supervisee brings will be incomplete and guarded. The more the supervisee feels judged by me then the more careful she will be to stay on 'safe' ground rather than risk areas where she suspects she may be working ineffectively or harmfully. However, if the supervisee feels fundamentally valued by me, then she can risk exploring the unknown, as in the following case:

> I want to *really* talk about my work with men. All I've ever done before is to gloss over my counselling with male clients. Although I've spoken about that work, I've never really said how frightened I am with men. It is as though I am constantly on my guard lest I arouse their disfavour. I guess I've never really faced this before, but I'm ready to do that now.

Those familiar with the person-centred approach will not be

surprised to find that *empathy* is my fourth condition. Empathy is the process by which I grasp the frame of reference of the supervisee and follow her personal meanings. When viewed from outside the person-centred approach, empathy is often regarded as a rather simple skill which every helper employs anyway. In reality, empathy is a broad concept incorporating many therapeutic processes including 'focusing'[2] (Gendlin, 1981) and even the skill which some call 'intuition' (Bowen, 1986).

In the context of the kind of 'support' offered by my commitment and genuine valuing of my supervisee, the 'challenges' offered through my empathy and congruence do not so readily arouse her defences. In the following extract from a supervision session the challenge is unequivocal but it is not experienced as threatening by the supervisee, Diane, *because* of the support she also feels within the relationship which we have established.

> *Diane*: He [*the client*] looks so distressed . . . so lost, and vulnerable. I feel that I just *have to* give him more frequent sessions. He is in desperate need . . . even though he doesn't quite feel it yet. What do you think?
>
> *Supervisor*: I 'think' you are over-involved.
>
> *[Pause]*
>
> *Diane*: You mean my 'stuff' is getting mixed up with his 'stuff'?
>
> *Supervisor*: Yes.
>
> *Diane*: I think at some level I knew that – I imagine that's really why I brought him up.
>
> *Supervisor*: Shall we explore it to see what's in it?

After this interchange I remember marvelling at how simple communication can be when the two people are not scared of each other. I am also aware, however, that such a lack of fear is not always easily achieved. I am distressed to discover that for some people I can be a frightening person until I have provided them with convincing evidence that their fear is misplaced.

The establishing of a healthy supervision relationship is a *necessary* condition for adequate work. However, once that relationship is established it is not in order for me to ignore it – relationships of any kind require maintenance.

## Keeping the supervision relationship healthy

There are all sorts of restrictive norms which can creep into a supervision relationship and smother it. The supervisee may be seeking to win my approval and consequently conceals elements of her practice about which she is doubtful. In other cases, perhaps it is I who have an overpowering need to be liked which results in my offering the supervisee 'support' but avoiding challenge. Or perhaps

I am so insecure that I become too 'distant' and set up an unnecessary 'transference' within the relationship which is thus prevented from developing a spirit of supportive challenge at all.

Both I and my supervisee need to take active steps to avoid the establishing of these cancerous restrictive norms. If we both feel a commitment to voice difficulties as they arise then that will contribute to the health of our supervision relationship. However, restrictive norms tend to develop in quiet, unobtrusive ways – often the dis-ease is well established before either of us is aware of a need to attend to the relationship. In just the same way as with relationships between partners, my supervisee and I may not be aware of the problem until our relationship is in crisis.

One way to avoid this creeping paralysis is to build into our supervision contract regular 'time-outs'. A 'time-out' in sport is

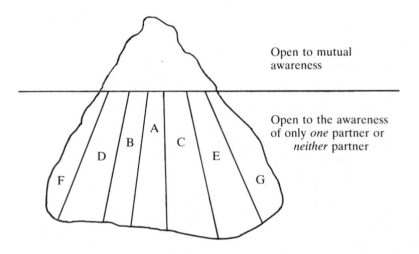

A: *Unclarified differences of opinion about the aims and practice of counselling and supervision.*
B: *The counsellor's unvoiced reactions to the supervisor.*
C: *The supervisor's unvoiced reactions to the counsellor.*
D: *The counsellor's unexpressed assumptions about the supervisor.*
E: *The supervisor's unexpressed assumptions about the counsellor.*
F: *The counsellor's unexamined assumptions about how the supervisor experiences her (the counsellor's) behaviour.*
G: *The supervisor's unexamined assumptions about how the counsellor experiences her (the supervisor's) behaviour.*

Figure 8.1  *The unspoken relationship*

when one team calls a temporary halt to the game to devote a little time to looking at its process. Similarly, the supervisee and I, even though we are not aware of difficulties in our relationship, can devote some time to examining what I like to call 'the unspoken relationship' between us (see Mearns and Dryden, 1990: Chapter 10). Although 'iceberg' analogies are ubiquitous in literature on conscious and unconscious experience, the representation in Figure 8.1 is a simple way to depict some aspects of the 'unspoken relationship' which I have found not infrequently develops between myself and my supervisees.

The following extract is taken from the tape of a supervision session where the supervisor (myself) and counsellor, Mary, discovered that our unspoken relationship contained incorrect assumptions which might well have led to restrictive norms creeping into our working relationship if we had not managed to unearth them.

*Mary*: I feel I am doing well.

*Supervisor*: I feel you are doing well too.

*Mary*: But I wasn't doing so well with Bill [*a client*].

*Supervisor*: I thought you were – you were really creative and flexible in your working with him.

*Mary*: Yes, I know . . . you said that at the time. But . . . well . . . I was a bit foolhardy with him, wasn't I . . .? I mean I got away with it – it worked out OK, but I took terrible risks – like when I accepted his wish to involve his wife, even though I had no idea what I was doing.

*Supervisor*: That surprises me – that wasn't how I saw it at all. I know you were on new ground working in that kind of way, but it seemed to me that you had a strong sense that that was the right way to go. It seemed OK to me.

*Mary*: You really felt that . . . at the time?

*Supervisor*: Yes. Like you, I had no idea where it would go, but I felt you were functioning quite fully and creatively.

*Mary*: You didn't feel I was a bit out of control?

*Supervisor*: No, I didn't. Certainly you were working in ways which were new to you and in that sense you couldn't predict what would happen, but I was following it closely and it was clear to me that you weren't over-involved or anything like that.

*Mary*: Are you sure you felt OK about it?

*Supervisor*: Of course I am sure – I wouldn't say it otherwise. Looking back on it, do *you* think you were over-involved?

*Mary*: No, but I was sure you did.

*Supervisor*: Why?

*Mary*: Partly because I knew it was the kind of judgement others might make – and partly because you were following it so closely – I thought that meant you had suspicions about me.

*Supervisor*: Maybe we should have talked like this at the time?

*Mary*: Yeah.

In this extract the misunderstanding which has arisen was partly due to Mary's vulnerability in relation to the very demanding case in which she was involved, but it also stemmed from her previous experience of others' judgements and her expectation that such judgement would fall upon her even in her supervision relationship with me. That assumption led to her misinterpretation of my close monitoring. If the health of the supervision relationship is to be maintained it is crucial that important misunderstandings like these are clarified before they spawn other spurious assumptions and soon create restrictive norms within the relationship. As well as helping to maintain the health of the relationship, the clarification of such a misunderstanding also offers learning for each of the parties involved. After the above interaction Mary was able to make therapeutic use for herself of her discovery that her previous experience of judgementalism in relationships still had a profound effect upon her, while I noted that I had not been sufficiently clear to Mary on how I was experiencing her work with the client.

## Critical issues in supervision

The supervision relationship is the vehicle which permits the counsellor to explore and develop his counselling. The emphasis in the first half of this chapter has been on creating and maintaining the kind of relationship which helps the counsellor to voice his difficulties without fear or inhibition. In the second half I shall look at a few of those difficulties that I have found recur in supervision and which might be described as 'critical issues'. I am conscious at this point of moving from what feels like fairly solid ground to terrain which often seems something of a minefield.

### Dealing with self-doubt
One question which can lie at the very core of the counsellor and which will threaten to undermine his whole practice is 'Am I any good at this?' This is such a fundamental and potentially self-destructive question that most counsellors can only bring it to supervision once a high level of trust has been established. It is a question which is best addressed during training supervision. Training should be a delightfully free time – a time when the counsellor can allow himself to be 'dreadful', 'hopeless', and express all the other archetypal fears which inevitably haunt the beginner. I encourage training supervisees to allow themselves to be 'learners who can make mistakes' and to take risks in exposing their work through making and sharing audio tapes of their actual counselling sessions. The hidden curriculum of sharing tapes is the way it can help the counsellor to dispel some of the self-doubt which may be

festering so long as he knows his practice has not been viewed by others.

Self-doubt during training is to be expected, but what if it occurs in the experienced worker? The following extract from a supervision tape with the counsellor, Shelley, shows just how painful self-doubt can be. The issue arose in the context of a 'time-out' during which I was voicing a little uneasiness in relation to the work we had been doing in our first few months:

*Supervisor*: We have been very busy – we've kept in touch with all your work, and looked at lots of issues . . . but I have a strange sense that we have been working very much on the surface – looking at the technical aspects of your work without really getting to grips with . . . something.

*Shelley*: Yes . . . without looking at the *real* question – the real *scary* question.

[*Long silence*]

*Shelley*: One of the reasons I came to you as a supervisor was that you were unconnected with my own counselling approach – you were an 'outsider' – so I could let you know me. The people around me would be too threatened if they realized just how despairing I am about my work. Every working day is lived at two levels – the superficial 'how clever I am to get that client to do exactly the right exercise at the right time' and the deeper voice in the back of my head – 'You are a fraud – you can't really help people – you just play powerful games with them and make them *think* they've been helped.' Every day is agony as that doubt eats away at my insides. Sometimes I'm sure my clients must see it – I feel hollow inside.

I remember the feeling of 'tightness' I had at this point in our session. I suspect I had been holding my breath for several minutes as Shelley finally expressed her self-doubt. I felt a mixture of awe that she was taking that huge step, and also a measure of apprehension as I suspected that the 'hollowness' she was experiencing might require more in-depth therapeutic work than our supervision contract could provide.

Shelley and I soon established separate supervision and therapy contracts. I find it perfectly feasible to carry both these roles simultaneously, but it is necessary to separate the contracts, else supervision tends to lose out to the more personally demanding needs of therapy.

*Counsellor 'under-involvement'*

One of the responsibilities I feel as a supervisor is to help the counsellor to ensure that the work he is doing with clients is indeed within the boundaries of 'counselling'. Hence I will be prepared to challenge him when he appears to be 'over-involved' with clients. But a much more difficult boundary is 'under-involvement': where the counsellor is not getting involved enough with the client. Over-involvement can be dramatic but it is much easier to bring someone back from that point than it is to help him to become more fully involved.

Under-involvement may be symptomatic of a counsellor who is in crisis himself – a crisis of a slow 'creeping' kind, but running quite deep. For instance, the counsellor may be keeping himself very hidden because he does not trust himself, or because what the client represents is existentially fearful to him, or perhaps because he is under severe stress. In any event, the counsellor who habitually does not give enough back to clients represents a considerable problem for the supervisor. One of the most difficult cases of under-involvement which I have encountered as a supervisor is described in the following notes which are pieced together from different sessions.

- I can't fathom Jim [the counsellor] at all. He seems to keep his clients at arm's length and asks me what he should 'do' with them. It is as though they are objects to him rather than people. He can think about them only in 'diagnostic-treatment' terms.
- I feel even more worried about Jim. He just cannot empathize at all – even when he tries. He is quite ego-syntonic. After spending a long time on his work with an abused client he ended the session with a joke about her in which he referred to her as a 'silly bitch'. When I reacted to that he apologized and appeared very meek – he just switched in a flash.
- Today Jim described a new client who had been in a lot of distress in the first session. Jim said that he wanted to help her, but he felt 'paralysed'. He was really in torment as he spoke about this – he had 'wanted to help' but 'didn't know what to do'. Then he had decided to 'just sit back, smile, and look confident'.

It is with considerable embarrassment that I have to report that it took me two years to face facts which my clinical knowledge as a psychologist had been screaming out to me from the very beginning – that there was no way in which Jim could be a counsellor. His clinical diagnosis would be one of 'personality disorder' – a way of being which is more likely to be abusive with clients than helpful. Jim is no longer a counsellor, but I cannot take credit for that good judgement because I was caught up in that common pattern of trying to 'help' him. I would have been more useful to his clients and to him if I had followed my intuition and challenged him very early. Counsellor under-involvement is sometimes born of a simple lack of confidence or a temporary paralysis which can be a phase within training when the counsellor is trying not to do the 'wrong' things and cannot quite think what the 'right' things are. But at other times it is symptomatic of a deep-seated pathology which can be just as dangerous for clients as the counsellor who is ostensibly 'over-involved'.

### Counsellor over-involvement

Helping the counsellor to identify examples of his over-involvement is one of the most important functions of the supervisor. By its very nature over-involvement is something which the counsellor cannot readily identify without help. It seems to him that he is just doing what is 'necessary' for the client. The supervisor's objectivity, combined with his willingness to challenge, is vital because over-involvement renders the counsellor blind. However, as a supervisor, I still do not find it a simple matter to spot examples of over-involvement in my supervisees. It is easy to identify over-involvement in retrospect, but while it is happening it is difficult to distinguish from 'full involvement'. I would want my supervisees to be fully involved with their clients, but where exactly is that boundary? Sometimes my supervisee's language presents clues for the detection of over-involvement. For example, where the counsellor gets into an *over-protective* relationship with the client, her language can give her away, as in the following references made by one counsellor about her client: 'the poor thing – she has been through an awful lot you know'/'she really needs someone to care for her'/'I really don't see how she has managed to cope'/'I just had to take her home with me – she had nowhere to go'/'I haven't said *that* to her yet – she couldn't really take that right now'.

However, even with a glaring example like this, it is not easy to challenge over-protectiveness effectively. The counsellor is emotionally involved with the client and as such will be ready to defend her view of her client forcefully. This situation always feels to me as though I am challenging another reality – a reality shared by the counsellor who needs to protect the client and the client who likes to be protected. I am the outsider – and who is to say that my reality is the one which is right? In response to my attempt at what I thought was a 'gentle' challenge, the counsellor in the above example said:

> What do you mean 'over-protective'? What am I expected to do – sit back and nod gratuitously while this woman has emotional lumps knocked off her by her husband? You can call me 'over-protective', but I must say that I find your passivity to be positively *abusive* of my client!

I felt abject horror and fell silent as I faced this label of 'abusive'. As a male therapist constantly confronting the effects of the abusiveness of my gender it was a terrible prospect to face the possibility of my own abusiveness, even if I did not believe it.

Goodness knows how such a clash of realities can ever be adequately resolved. In this particular example my supervisee saw my torment and realized that she really had hit me hard. While I was temporarily immobilized she was able to open out the whole issue.

The most obviously abusive form of over-involvement is sexual. Indeed, when these instances are examined from the client's perspective, the term 'over-involvement' is nothing more than a sexist euphemism – more appropriate words are 'sexual harassment' or 'sexual abuse'. The sexual harassment or sexual abuse of a client can take many forms, ranging from pushing the client to talk about her sexual experiences through sexual touching to outright sexual intercourse. In my experience, the one element which is common to all these different forms of abuse is that the counsellor justifies his behaviour as 'helpful' for the client. A breakthrough for me in understanding situations of sexual harassment or sexual abuse was to learn that the whole issue has little to do with sexual feeling but a lot to do with *power*. Hence, many examples of abuse do not appear to contain an overt sexual component but involve the male counsellor's dominance and the client eventually feels abused or 'uncomfortable'. A classic scenario of this form of sexual abuse is where the female client feels mystified by the 'wisdom' and 'power' of the male counsellor and indeed may imbue him with spiritual or mystical powers. This kind of working can have quite dramatic results for the client but it is also extremely difficult for her to find her own power and escape from the power of the counsellor. As a supervisor I find that this form of sexual abuse is very difficult to challenge because both the client and the counsellor are caught up with the 'power' of the experience and may initially deny its abusive aspect. I can easily begin to feel that I am the 'odd one out' in questioning such an obviously 'powerful' therapeutic experience. However, although I was reticent in earlier years, I have now seen sufficient examples of clients who have been abused by psychiatrists and counsellors that I tend to err on the side of safety.

In one case a new supervisee, Patrick, described his work with the client, Yvonne, thus:

> I doubt if I've ever worked so fully with a client as I have with Yvonne. I seem to be breaking personal barriers all the time. From being someone who was a bit 'stiff' about physical contact with clients I am becoming so much more open and responsive. In one recent meeting I found myself offering to give her a massage. She was so stuck, so tense, so needing to

> express all the feelings within her – yet they just wouldn't come out, no matter what she tried. In the massage I was careful to avoid her sexual areas, but I could feel every ounce of her tension with my fingertips. Slowly and gently she let her feeling out – it had been pent up for so long that it came out as screaming.

I felt that he was only guessing about Yvonne's experience rather than empathizing with her. After two sessions of tentatively expressing my discomfort, but seeming to get nothing back from Patrick except about the 'power' of his work with Yvonne, I confronted the situation by instructing him to stop working with Yvonne on the grounds that he was sexually over-involved. This was an incredibly difficult thing to do. I felt I was going out on a limb with my judgement. All sorts of questions flashed before me as if to get me to recant: 'Am I really *that* sure this man is over-involved? Am I over-reacting because of *earlier* experiences with sexual abuse? Am I over-reacting because *I am too stiff* as a counsellor to work in physical ways? Am I endangering our whole relationship?'

If Patrick had come back firmly, I'm not sure that I could have held to my resolve at that moment. In fact, he responded quite meekly and showed that at some level he too was worried about his involvement with Yvonne. Within a few weeks Patrick had stopped counselling altogether and Yvonne was with a woman counsellor who spoke with me about Yvonne's experience with Patrick. The following is Yvonne's account of the massage experience.

> I felt a whole mixture of feelings towards him – none of which I could talk about easily. I felt he was really trying to help me; I felt he was overpowering me; and I felt simultaneously attracted and scared of him. When he offered to massage me it made sense because I was so tense, but I was really scared – I just couldn't say 'No', though now I wish I had. While he was touching me I felt completely at his mercy. In the end I broke down. I felt unbelievably vulnerable – it was as though this man was saying to me 'I can help you if you give yourself to me'.

These parallel accounts illustrate Patrick's over-involvement and the sexual abuse of Yvonne. Patrick had very little insight about how Yvonne was experiencing events and Yvonne for her part felt immobilized by conflicting feelings.

Although Patrick was no longer counselling after this incident, I was still his supervisor and while the boundary between supervision and therapy would become blurred I still had a responsibility to Patrick until he could properly engage the underlying issues for him. In a situation like this it is too easy to feel protective of the client and angry at the counsellor. Following an instance of sexual over-involvement the counsellor is going to need me more than ever before – it would be a pity if I had aligned with the client in such a way as to exclude the counsellor.

*Where the counsellor is more effective than the supervisor*
I have left this issue to the end because personally I find it more important even than the supervisor's role with respect to over-involvement. One of the most difficult tasks for me as a supervisor is to facilitate my supervisee's development when she is more accomplished than myself.

I think that one of the things which helps me as a supervisor is my very clear understanding of my strengths and limitations as a counsellor. I consider myself to be a dedicated and extremely committed counsellor – the degree of my commitment at times amazes me. I also think that a strong point in my work is my willingness to look at my own process as well as the client's, for that so often is the key to successful working. Furthermore, I think I am particularly effective with the client who, in conventional psychiatric terms, would be deemed 'profoundly disturbed'. Similarly, I suspect I feel more comfortable than most counsellors in working with the suicidal client. However, on the other hand, I think I am pretty 'stiff' as a counsellor and not nearly as imaginative or creative as many of my colleagues. Over the years I have studiously avoided developing clever counselling 'techniques'. I have justified that to myself of course, but basically it stems from a fundamental uneasiness I have with taking on that much responsibility *for* the client. In other words, my appraisal of myself as a counsellor has positives, negatives and some 'undecideds'. As a supervisor, one of the most important things for me to remember is that my supervisee is a different person from me: it is not my job to constrain my supervisee to model his work on myself. There may be aspects of my working which he chooses to adopt, but in most areas he will have his own style, and in some instances his functioning will be superior to mine. I think it is most important for a supervisor and supervisee to discuss issues like this as an aspect of their work together.

A recent experience which emphasized my supervisee's superiority in that regard leaves me with a mixture of embarrassment and also some glee and self-mocking. One of my training supervisees gave me regular tapes of her work with a client, George. Over a period of more than a year I listened to these interminable tapes of George and his counsellor. I was able to offer all sorts of fragments of feedback but more than anything else what I kept saying was 'Let's push George' – 'How about using yourself more fully?' – 'How about challenging George a bit more?' After many tapes I challenged the counsellor to terminate with George on the grounds that they seemed well and truly 'stuck'. I felt that this was rather a radical suggestion but also that I could trust the counsellor to treat it as a very firm challenge which might help her to focus on what *she* wanted to do. As is often the case with such challenges I felt she had the strength to say 'No' if that was what she felt. What actually happened was that I did not get any more tapes of George for quite a while until one arrived quite unexpectedly some months later. On this tape 'George' was quite unrecognizable. This 'George' was solid and clear about himself. He could talk about his feelings rather than stutter about them. He could speak openly on his thoughts and feelings about the work he and his counsellor had been doing for some 18 months. In other words, my supervisee's patience and tolerance, so much in excess of my own, had been crucially important for George who had needed just those qualities for his slow and tentative emergence. I would have been absolutely no use as a counsellor for George – I would probably have threatened the hell out of him. It is with a smile that I acknowledge the importance for my supervisee of retaining her own power in relation to me, and forgive myself for being human.

### Notes

1 Where work with supervisees is extensively quoted or used in this chapter, those supervisees have been consulted and in some cases the presentation is also disguised to preserve anonymity.

2 As it is used here, 'focusing' is a technical term arising from the work of Eugene Gendlin (1981, 1984). It denotes a process of relaxing and attending to feelings and sensations which are on the very edge of awareness and in this way becoming aware of underlying tensions, conflict or meanings.

### References

Bowen, M. (1986) 'Personality differences and person-centered supervision', *Person-Centered Review*, 1 (3): 291–309.

Gendlin, E.T. (1981) *Focusing*. New York: Bantam.

Gendlin, E.T. (1984) 'The client's client: the edge of awareness', in R.F. Levant and J.M. Shlien (eds), *Client-Centered Therapy and the Person-Centered Approach*. New York: Praeger.

Mearns, D. and Dryden, W. (eds) (1990) *Experiences of Counselling in Action*. London: Sage.

Mearns, D. and Thorne, B. (1988) *Person-Centred Counselling in Action*. London: Sage.

# 9 On Being a Supervisee

## Judy Moore

I currently work as a student counsellor and have done so for nearly five years, first of all as a trainee, then as a part-time sessional counsellor and subsequently on a half-time contract. Before I undertook a person-centred training in counselling and psychotherapy in September 1985 I had always worked in the field of education. I have taught a variety of courses for the Open University since 1982 and currently tutor a course in Women's Studies. I am therefore accustomed to working in a fairly circumscribed way where I am relatively in control of the circumstances in which I try to facilitate my students' understanding of a specific body of material. By contrast, I am a relative newcomer to the open-endedness of working with individuals in terms of their personal growth. I am gradually learning not to expect quick and tangible results from my counselling work, but I still incline towards impatience. At the beginning of my training I was seeing on average three clients a week and now I see between 14 and 17 clients a week during the university term and half that number out of term time. Over this period I have had two individual supervisors and been a participant in two supervision groups.

The key issue for me in supervision is how to use the time in a way that is both engaging and constructive. It is difficult enough to talk about one's own experience, but in trying to represent an absent third person (i.e. the client) there is even more scope for inaccuracy or evasion. My experience of supervision to date has involved a search for how to keep something *living* in the session in which both my supervisor or my supervision group and I can feel truly engaged. Another important issue for me has been how to work out what is going on in my supervisor or in other individuals in my supervision group and how open I can allow myself to be in their presence. This might mean working out their expectations, their prejudices or assumptions, or any significant knowledge which they might be withholding. My imaginative reconstructions of other people's realities have led to my making a number of mistakes for the sake of holding on to a sense of my own power in different supervisory contexts. The issue of power and empowerment has been and remains a very problematic one for me as a supervisee.

What I propose to look at here is my changing experience and perception of supervision within four different contexts and how these have contributed to my present beliefs about its use.

## Individual supervision as a trainee

A requirement of the course in counselling and psychotherapy that I began in September 1985 was that participants should both be seeing clients and receiving regular supervision throughout the training. I had been seeing my first supervisor for psychotherapy for a year before the beginning of the course and it was agreed that she should become my supervisor. She is not person-centred by training but is a very experienced eclectic therapist whose focus has always been to help me to find my *own* strength and solutions. The transition from therapy to supervision was non-problematic and basically involved a widening of focus to include clients and client-related issues in what we discussed in our sessions.

It is only in retrospect that I can appreciate how simple my approach to being supervised was in those early days. I believed in a very uncomplicated way that whatever was most significant would emerge in the course of the session and it always did. It never occurred to me to ask for advice: as far as I was concerned I was either in a counselling relationship that was working or else I was experiencing difficulty in relating to a client and it was that difficulty I needed to look at. I took this attitude for granted because my supervisor always encouraged me to look at myself in relation to any client issue and the precedent for self-exploration established over a year of therapy meant that if I was experiencing difficulty with a client she would very quickly bring the focus back to me.

During my training I experienced difficulties with clients in a number of specific areas that I can recall. For example, I found it difficult to accept women who had taken on a traditional domestic role. In the early stages of my training I would have been intolerant of a mature female student who was experiencing difficulty in balancing study with her domestic responsibilities. I am quite certain that my supervisor would have handled this particular case by bringing me back to the intolerance and helping me to look at where it was coming from *in me*. Most of the difficulties I experienced in those early days were in relation to acceptance and came from unresolved aspects of my past. We worked on my early relationships so extensively both in supervision and out of it (I had many additional sessions of therapy both during my training and since its completion) that I hope and believe I am now much less likely to bring unresolved personal material to the counselling relationship.

Another aspect of supervision was related to the development of my own facilitative skills. I know that I have been very much influenced by my experience of both my first and my current individual supervisors' accurate and appropriate empathy and their high level of acceptance. I don't believe that my first supervisor and I ever discussed the development of empathy or acceptance in a theoretical way but I was simply learning from my experience of *her* practice. I also felt that she was very much engaged with me as a person and never gave the impression of being bored. Always we were working with something living, i.e. my feelings, and I was much less inhibited in this relationship than in my other supervisory contexts where I have become confused by believing that I should be talking about clients in a particular way or somehow trying to be a different person from who I am.

My relationship with my first supervisor was initially a very simple one in so far as I believed that ultimately she knew best. I felt empowered in my work and in the rest of my life because I felt both understood and accepted. Within our relationship, however, she was more powerful because I was more 'known' and therefore more vulnerable. Subsequently, as I came to know and trust myself more, I became a great deal more questioning of her assumptions and insights. What this more questioning attitude means is that it seems unlikely that ever again could I be in such an uncomplicated individual supervisory relationship as I was during my training.

## Group supervision as a trainee

My experience of group supervision as a trainee in some ways shook the confidence that I was building up in individual supervision. We were a group of six women and two men who met with a male supervisor for a whole day every month during the 2½-year training period. The immediate difference for me in being in a group was that I now had nine potential models of person-centredness. Clearly our group supervisor was the most experienced and therefore the most powerful member of the group and it was his behaviour that I chose to emulate.

This was a disastrous mistake. In an essay that I wrote towards the end of the course I analysed the leadership styles of the four course staff members and defined my group supervisor as conforming to John Heron's 'six dimensions' of facilitator style (Heron, 1977) in the following ways: that he was predominantly non-directive, non-interpretative, unstructuring, cathartic, non-confronting and non-disclosing. It is this last dimension that I now see as particularly problematic, although it would be much more accurate to say that my group supervisor was selectively disclosing rather than non-disclosing. He would, for example, demonstrate concern and compassion but not irritation or impatience. As I am often irritated and impatient, this caused me some difficulty, given the fact that I regarded him as a 'model' of how I should be. I might just about have managed to reveal impatience or irritation with a client, but it would have been unthinkable for me to reveal negative feelings about anyone within the supervision group. Our supervisor demonstrated very caring attitudes and was obviously very sensitive, but he was often silent and sometimes gave the impression of being disengaged. Because I recognized his sensitivity, I imagined that the silence concealed an ocean of raging emotions which he was somehow, with tremendous skill and self-control, managing to contain. My experience was further complicated by the fact that my attitude towards him involved some projection of protective attitudes that I had held towards my own father. Basically this meant that I needed to intuit what was going on behind the silence and to support him in making everything run in the caring and controlled way I imagined he wanted the group to run.

As a result of all this, I developed a fantasy that to be person-centred was to be very caring and also very restrained. In effect, although I did not identify it at the time, in trying to fulfil this fantasy, I was learning how *not* to be congruent. I was deliberately concealing certain aspects of my experiencing because I wanted to attain to an ideal considerably far removed from my real self. This inevitably coloured the client material that I brought to the group and how I presented myself as a counsellor.

At the beginning of each supervision day we would spend some time saying how we all were and then we would work out an agenda. Some people would have specific clients that they wanted to discuss and others might wish to look at particular issues – for example, counselling clients with eating disorders or working with couples. Sometimes we would bring along tapes of counselling sessions and listen to and comment on each other's work. One of the most helpful things we did was to role-play, sometimes taking on the role of a client with whom we were having particular difficulty, while another member of the group would be the counsellor. The group was a valuable arena in which to consider a new way of working in the company of other individuals who were also experimenting with ways of being person-centred counsellors. It was a relief to learn that other people also got stuck and made mistakes and it was helpful to hear other people's comments on difficulties that I was experiencing. Our supervisor was both skilled and experienced and his insights into my work were particularly valuable. I trusted him and I appreciated his instigation of ways of working that were different from the very personal focus of my individual supervision.

The negative side of sharing my work with the group was that I became comparative and competitive. I found it very difficult to hold on to being myself when I could perceive that other people worked in very effective ways that were different from mine. I began to believe that, because they were different, everybody else was better than me. I could not have shared these feelings of inadequacy with the group for three reasons: (a) I was being competitive and therefore I would not have wanted to draw attention to my inadequacies; (b) I was irritated by another member of the group whose excessive self-denigration demanded a lot of reassurance and I didn't want to get into that particular game; (c) I was afraid of being different by giving expression to negative feelings other than those that related to grief. It is interesting to me in retrospect that of the four basic negative emotions (anger, grief, fear and jealousy) identified by Elisabeth Kübler-Ross (1988), I believed that only grief was acceptable in the supervision group. I can see now that the three reasons I give above for not expressing my feelings of inadequacy involve the suppression of anger (b), fear (c) and jealousy (a).

I was not the only person in the group who censored their expression of negative feelings. It was a safe and helpful, but sometimes a rather 'dead', place. It was most alive when we were actively recreating a particular scenario with a client and new insights were emerging as we worked. At other times it came to life when somebody was engaged in working through a personal issue, generally helped by the group supervisor and sometimes by the rest of us. However, suppressed negativity got in the way a lot of the time and confrontation between us was very rare. Many issues between us as individuals were left unresolved and difficulties built up as time went on. My own immediate outlet was to explode at the end of each day when I got home. This meant that, as each supervision day wore on, I would bottle up each feeling that I regarded as being 'inappropriate' to the caring, compassionate human being that I 'ought' to be. I can remember trying to emulate our supervisor's carefully controlled gestures in a way that now seems to me completely absurd. Inside, however, I was often a seething mass of frustration, longing for the release at the end of the day.

I now recognize that the group was limited by the excessive focus of all its participants on empathy and acceptance at the expense of congruence. This coloured how I tried to be as a human being in person-centred circles and I'm sure that it also influenced the way I worked. When I look at the videos of myself counselling as a trainee it is like watching half a person. My vitality, so much present in individual supervision, is missing as it was often missing in the supervision group. I wish that I had had the courage to be more honest, but I think this would have been impossible while my main object was to protect our supervisor and make things go in the carefully controlled way I imagined he wanted them to go. I would now try to trust *myself* and my own experiencing a great deal more than I ever did then because I believe that, in trying to be restrained, I really held myself back in terms of my own personal and professional development.

## Current individual supervision

I have been having individual supervision with my current supervisor five times a term for five terms. I have known him throughout my training, both as a colleague at the student counselling service at which we work and as one of my course trainers. I noted in my essay on the leadership styles of the four trainers that he was the one on to whom I projected most of their manipulative power. This remains a key issue in supervision as I still experience him as both powerful and potentially manipulative as well as very empathic and supportive.

I experience my supervisor as powerful in relation to me for several reasons: he is older and more experienced than I am; he occupies a more senior and controlling position within the university and has access to information that I don't have; he was originally one of my trainers and has experience of me in a variety of vulnerable emotional states whereas I do not have such extensive knowledge of his vulnerability; he is better versed than I am in person-centred theory; he has a deeper and broader understanding of human nature than I have; he is less impatient than I am. I am quite surprised, given all these factors, that I don't feel more inadequate in supervision than I do and this I imagine derives partly from the fact that he is generally very affirming of what I am doing and because I also implicitly trust his acceptance of and goodwill towards me as a person.

There are three areas that I would currently regard as problematic for me in my relationship with my supervisor. The first relates to his access to information (including information that relates to the stability or otherwise of my job) about which I am curious. The giving and withholding of such information is very much within his power and I sometimes find myself speculating as to whether or not information is being withheld from me. Much of our contact outside supervision involves my observation of my supervisor as an administrator and a political manoeuverer in his position as a senior counsellor. I am then very aware of him devising plans and strategies. I tend to look *behind* what he does and says and it is difficult for me to abandon this mode in supervision. I also perceive him as a very competent individual who can function well on one level while concealing many different stresses and anxieties. This leads on to the second difficulty I have, which is that I suspect he is at times not entirely present in supervision, a suspicion that is occasionally fed by his stifled yawns or my awareness that he is currently involved in some taxing crisis or other. We have addressed the first of these issues and I now feel easier about asking for information; the second is currently more difficult for me, partly because it would involve me pressing my claim against (what I imagine to be) the overwhelming weight of his other concerns.

The third area of difficulty is one that is only just becoming clear to me as having been an issue, which relates to the fact that I was on maternity leave for the first term of the current academic year and have been trying to combine work with the pressures of caring for a young baby for the past two terms. As I am extremely conscientious, I would sooner have died than admit to the person who was responsible for employing me that I might be feeling the strain, particularly during the early and most difficult months. It was only ever my supervisor who introduced the concept of mother-hood into our sessions, implying, with what I regarded as surprising optimism, that this new role would deepen my understanding and therefore improve the quality of my work. In retrospect, I think that his positive attitude and apparent lack of anxiety was important in helping me to keep hold of my faith in my own ability, despite my inevitable doubts and fears.

In the light of this strategic withholding of some feelings that might have diminished my supervisor's faith in me as an employee, it is interesting to speculate as to how far my supervisor's occasional lack of presence in our sessions did indeed derive from his worries or from the fact that I may at times have been concealing my own most pressing concern. I do think that loss of energy in supervision is very much related to the concealment of feelings. Although I have focused on it here as an issue, I don't think in general I have consciously withheld very much in individual supervision. In fact, during this post-natal period I have been emotionally very open and, with my supervisor, almost without inhibition in revealing negative feelings either about clients or other issues that relate less directly to our own relationship.

With one client I had such strong negative feelings that I did my utmost to persuade her not to come back. What I found so irritating about her was that (a) she kept waiting for me to 'lead'; (b) she kept on telling me 'shocking' things for effect (looking at me carefully all the time for my response); (c) she told me (after much circumlocution on her part and massive probing on mine) that she was obsessed with a young man who was gay and pestered him constantly (my words); (d) she didn't want to look at herself in relation to any of this; (e) she lisped. After I had recounted all this, my supervisor said words to the effect of the following: 'What you are saying is that here is somebody whom you find irritating for a number of reasons, any of which may be triggering something that is more to do with you than with her.' He then fed back to me what I had said about her in a slightly altered and more generalized form, i.e. here was somebody that I could hardly bear to see again who was (a) passive and putting pressure on me to take responsibility for her; (b) trying to make some kind of an impact on me; (c) wouldn't take 'no' for an answer; (d) was not very self-aware; (e) and who gave the impression of being harmless and innocent but was actually affecting me in a very negative way. This version of the client instantly made me realize that what she had been doing was re-creating the quality of a very difficult relationship that I was currently experiencing in my own life. This was an absolute revelation and a very helpful one (though too late to be helpful to the client who came in that same day to cancel her next grudgingly given appointment). What this particular episode tells me is that there would have been no point in discussing the client without presenting her in terms of the very strong feelings of antipathy that she roused in me so that my supervisor could help me, in much the same way that my first supervisor would have done, to identify where those feelings were really coming from.

To talk about a client in terms of the feelings she is generating in me is to take a risk which I could only take if I felt wholly accepted by my supervisor. This is not to say that to give voice to my feelings in relation to the client will inevitably mean that those feelings will always be more to do with me than with the client. I assume that part of the skill of being a supervisor lies in identifying when the feelings of the supervisee might be usefully implemented in the counselling relationship, as in the following example. Much of one session was spent in my agonizing over the fact that I seemed to be spending a lot of time being irritated by or frustrated with clients. When we looked at a client by whom I was currently frustrated (someone who went round and round in circles going over the same material), my supervisor validated my feelings of frustration in relation to this particular client and suggested that I might trust myself to be more congruent. An interesting consequence of this supervision was that when I saw a client that afternoon by whom I was again feeling frustrated (because we seemed to be getting nowhere), but also sensing some hostility in her, I decided to address what was going on by asking if she did indeed feel annoyed with me. She agreed that she was annoyed because I had started the session a bit late. This was a most significant breakthrough as she has great difficulty in relationships because she finds it impossible to express negative feelings. I think that had we not looked at congruence in supervision, I would not have listened so carefully to my feeling of frustration, nor taken the risk of addressing the hostility.

It seems to me that, in general terms, I am using individual supervision whenever I come up against my own limitations in the counselling relationship. This might mean that negative feelings are getting in the way of acceptance and thus blocking the relationship. On a more simple level it might mean that I become stuck simply because I don't know enough about the culture or beliefs of individual clients. This has happened to me, for example, in relation to overseas students, with clients struggling over contradictions in their Christian faith and in relation to the compulsive nature of eating disorders. In each of these cases all I have needed is to be given information, which is helpful, but I would not regard the giving of information as an essential part of supervision.

I am often very tempted to ask for advice in supervision because I like quick 'solutions'. For example, because I know that my supervisor tends to put things very well, I'm often tempted to ask how he would suggest that I might word some delicate point that I want to raise with a client. I have, however, more than once found myself quite unable to transmit his phraseology to the client or something else has gone wrong in the transaction. I assume that this is partly because the effect is rather like a weak student trying to pass off a secondary text as her own words in an essay. In other words, that it must jar against my usual style. On the other hand, it might equally or also be that between my narration of somebody else's experience and my supervisor's interpretation and response, something vital has been lost. At heart I know that my supervisor can only enable me to find my own way with the client and that advice is only an apparent leap forward and more likely than not a leap in the wrong direction. We have discussed this, but, while knowing that it probably is a non-productive direction, my impulse to ask what *he* would do is still very strong and I would be furious if I knew that he were deliberately withholding an answer!

Knowledge and understanding are extremely important to me on a cognitive as well as an affective level and it is a source of some relief to me that my supervisor does not dismiss my questioning or curiosity as a defence. I simply want to know everything, whether it is the truth of my own or my client's experiencing, how secure my job is or what is the most productive way of using supervision. I regard my supervisor as a means by which I can achieve more knowledge and therefore it seems to me valid to ask questions. I know that supervision is helpful to me in making an affective shift forwards into greater self-knowledge and a cognitive shift towards greater general knowledge. I can also see that to leave unasked questions around the relationship with my supervisor will only frustrate me and be counter-productive to the development of my patience and understanding.

Supervision is for me a source of empowerment in so far as it clarifies what is going on for me in difficult and confusing counselling relationships. It is giving me an increasing trust in my own experiencing and I really value my supervisor's intelligence and empathy in helping me move forward in my understanding. I am absolutely certain that I work better with clients as a result of supervision. The supervisory relationship will probably remain to some extent problematic because of the imbalance of power within it, but I find this quite interesting and thought-provoking and I like the challenge and stimulus it provides.

### Current group supervision

Group supervision remains in many ways a difficult area for me, although I can find it very stimulating and helpful. To be fully met by, engaged with and empowered by a group of people seems an almost impossible ideal, though one for which I believe it is worth striving.

The staff of the university counselling service sometimes meets as a group as large as twelve, but more often it is a group of six to eight. We meet weekly as a staff group and three times a term are joined by our consultant psychiatrist and a medical practitioner from the University Health Centre. The meetings are therefore of varying degrees of formality, depending on how many of us are there and whether or not we have visitors present. The meetings are used for the dissemination of information and for us to talk about personal issues as well as for supervision. Although we are theoretically a peer group, there is in fact a hierarchical structure based on positions of seniority within the service. The fact that some people carry more authority than others, together with difficulties that exist between some individuals in the group, means that there can be considerable constraints in operation, although we are much more in the habit of looking at these constraints than we ever did in my training supervision group or when I was first in this particular group.

When I was first in this group I was a trainee and assumed that I should follow the practice of the others (only four people of the group I originally knew are still there) as they were all more experienced than I was. Negativity was rarely expressed and the habitual mode of client discussion was the 'case-study' mode, where the focus would be on the client rather than the relationship or the counsellor's feelings about the client. The group has since changed quite radically and feels to me much nearer to a peer group, with an influx of new person-centred blood, including some from my own training course and the one after mine. I feel much freer in this version of the group, but the problem of how to claim space and how to present myself and my clients remains.

In terms of its supervisory function, the group at present veers between the 'case-study' mode and the 'personal feeling' mode, the latter exemplified at a recent meeting by a colleague who began by saying, 'I'd like to talk about a client I'm frightened of'. Here was something real, i.e. the counsellor's fear, that we could all respond to and could feel engaged in looking at what it was in the client that made her afraid and what she could do about it. Sometimes it is really hard to know where members of the group are going with client issues that they raise, but as long as their feelings are acknowledged in relation to the issue then I find it possible to remain engaged with their exploration.

It is difficult to remember when the shift towards this more personal (and, to me, much more valuable) mode of client presentation came about, but I know that a significant breakthrough in my own case was when I had a profoundly suicidal client whose relentless negativity frequently drove me to despair. I would often see him just before our meetings and it was extremely helpful to be able to give voice to this despair and feel that it was heard by my colleagues. At other times I was frustrated by him, worried about the responsibility if he were to succeed in killing himself and, later in the year when he had moved on from feeling suicidal to feeling murderous, I was frightened of him. I expressed all of these feelings in our group supervision and it was invaluable in terms of my being able to stay with the client to have a supportive arena for such discharge. The insights of our consultant psychiatrist and the doctor who had contact with the client at the Health Centre were also important in helping me feel less alone with what seemed (but in fact turned out not to be) a hopeless case.

In the above example my feelings were so strong and so immediate that I did not stop to think about the 'appropriateness' of my method of presentation or even whether anybody was likely to be interested in what I had to say. Often, when I do stop to think, either about how I might respond to somebody else or whether or not I should bring up an issue that is bothering me, I become inhibited to the point of paralysis. This inhibition derives partly from a fear of being judged and relates to the fear of not being as good as everybody else that I experienced in my training group. I now regard myself as being deficient in two specific ways in my present supervision group: first, I often feel that I'm not as accepting as our two most senior and experienced practitioners, who both model an extraordinary benignity that can inhibit my own expression of negativity; secondly, I'm afraid that my empathy might be rather clumsy and I imagine that someone else would make a better response than mine.

I don't often express feelings of inadequacy in the group because I don't completely trust everyone present not to pass dismissive judgement on me. I know I would restrain myself from falling apart in the group in a way that I wouldn't restrain myself in individual supervision. Another current source of inhibition is that I have in the past expressed difficult feelings I have held towards other individuals in the group, probably more strongly than anybody else, and I feel rather reluctant to keep on being the person who is the first to express any negativity that is around. I can imagine addressing these sources of inhibition at some point as we have begun to look a great deal more at what is going on in the group, but to change entrenched patterns and to deal with each individual's difficulties with the group will inevitably take a long time.

Because we are limited to two hours a week, it is quite precious time, and what holds me back more than anything in the group is that I simply have enormous difficulty in claiming or intruding on what I regard as valuable space. How do I decide whether or not my impulse to respond to a colleague or my need to talk about a client or any other issue is more pressing than anyone else's? I think I am currently suffering from having been in too many groups that have been characterized by a powerful, withholding silence wherein I feel that the silence can only be broken by some momentous statement or response. I am really longing to be spontaneous and open and I hate my own paralysis. When, after a long silence, somebody begins to speak, then it is likely that my energy has begun to subside and I am sometimes merely parodying acceptance and empathy while my real self moves further and further away from the person to whom I am pretending to respond. It seems that it is by such a process happening to a number of participants in the group that it becomes dead and, in effect, a parody of its own person-centred beliefs.

My current supervision group is basically a very supportive one, but I am quite certain that we all experience difficulties with it. I have merely given some of my own difficulties here, none of which I see as insurmountable. I really value the group and the insights that come from different perspectives within it and I think it is worth our working collectively towards more openness and trust, as I feel we *are* doing, albeit in a rather slow and sometimes convoluted way.

## Conclusion

I am conscious that my needs in supervision have changed over the past five years and that the whole issue is becoming more complex as I am becoming more self-aware and more sensitive to what is going on in other individuals. At the beginning of my training I needed a lot of safety to begin to allow myself (and therefore my clients) to get in touch with a wider range of feelings. Accurate empathy and acceptance were the starting points and remain important, but congruence and a sense of being engaged with as a whole person and feeling free to engage spontaneously with others have since become more significant issues for me. It seems to me that it must require enormous skill on the part of an individual supervisor to know which level of response is the most appropriate to move the supervisee forward at any given time. In a group the possibilities for response and stimulation are multiplied, but so are the possibilities for misunderstanding, comparison, paralysis and frustration. Whatever the context, I know that supervision is most productive when I simply stay with what I am feeling in relation to the client or any other issue, when I have the courage to be myself and when a full range of my own needs is met by my supervisor or supervision group. It is by this means that I am empowered as an individual to find my own solutions and enabled to reach new levels of self-awareness so that I am more and more able to stay with clients at deeper levels of exploration.

## References

Heron, John (1977) *Dimensions of Facilitator Style*. University of Surrey, Guildford: Human Potential Research Project.

Kübler-Ross, Elisabeth (1988) 'Death, the final stage of growth', in Stanislav Grof (ed.), *Human Survival and Consciousness Evolution*. Albany: State University of New York Press, pp. 274–85.

# PART 3   TRAINING COUNSELLOR TRAINERS AND SUPERVISORS

## 10   The Training of Counsellor Trainers and Supervisors

### Petrūska Clarkson and Maria Gilbert

**Introduction**

When a person takes the step from working as a counsellor to working, in addition, as a trainer and/or supervisor, a substantial shift is required in his or her frame of reference. This shift involves a change of role, an increased field of responsibility, the acquisition of a different range of skills and personal demands of another order. The trainer and supervisor no longer have responsibility only to their clients (for whom they usually take full responsibility) but also to the clients of their trainees and supervisees whom they may never meet.

All good practitioners do not make competent trainers and/or supervisors. Training and supervision should not *necessarily* be seen as a career progression. Indeed, excellent counsellors may do the work so well and with such practised and habitual ease that they no longer consciously think about the steps involved in the successful execution of the task. 'They are competent, but they are *unconsciously* competent, and that's what makes them poor instructors . . . they cannot communicate to a trainee – to an individual who is *consciously* incompetent – about what it takes to do the job' (Robinson, 1974: 538, our italics). Good trainers or supervisors need to be consciously competent – aware of why and what they are doing and able to convey it clearly and effectively.

Competence is here defined as being able to meet the demands of the task both objectively (assessed by others) and subjectively (assessed by self). Incompetence is here understood, not as a derogatory term, but as a descriptive indication that further development is required in order to meet objective competency criteria. We furthermore identify 'pseudo-competency' where indi-

viduals may appear *objectively* to be able to do the task compe-
tently, but *subjectively* do not experience the confidence that they
will be able to do it consistently well without severe anxiety and
without strain or undue energy drainage afterwards.

Some people have qualities that particularly suit them to the
training field. These may include an ability to hold the total map of
the material to be taught yet attend to detail, a logical deductive
approach, a preference for working with larger groups, the capacity
to convey complex material in a simple manner and the flexibility
to respond to people with widely differing learning styles. Other
people may be better suited as supervisors and possess qualities
such as a finely tuned intuition, a preference for the greater
intimacy of individual or small-group situations, the capacity to
relate to a large number of divergent options and an ability to see
the whole or gestalt in a particular situation. Training and supervision competencies do of course overlap, but there is a fine
distinction between these two areas which results in differing
emphases.

The rest of this chapter will cover guiding core concepts in the
training of counsellor trainers and supervisors followed by more
extensive discussion of three identifiable, but not necessarily always
separable, phases in the development of trainers and supervisors.
The final section briefly indicates the content of supervisor and
trainer training.

## Core concepts in the training of trainers and supervisors of counsellors

### Fostering the natural creative drive in human beings to learn and develop

We hold a basic assumption that human beings have, along with
sexual and aggressive drives, an equally important instinctual drive
for creativity, evolutionary development, the achievement of competence and the striving for excellence. This instinctual force has
been given the name of *Physis* (Aristotle, *Phys*. 193a, 9). We
therefore see the essential task in the training of counsellor trainers
and supervisors to be in the spirit of 'education' – the root of which
means to 'lead forth'. Accepting that some knowledge and skills
need to be imparted from the outside, we work to encourage the
natural learner in every trainee trainer or supervisor to 'come forth'
or develop. We see the primary task of educators of whatever
description to be this process of 'leading forth' while providing
external guidance and direction when required.

We also take seriously the research which suggests that teacher expectation can have a determining influence on the performance of students. Rosenthal and Jacobson (1968) found that students respond differentially to teachers' expectations of them even when these are unvoiced. When teachers believed students were unintelligent and could not learn, the children responded with lowered performance, no matter what their original intellectual endowment. Positive expectations influenced the students' performance in positive ways even if they were not academically gifted.

It has also been our experience that individuals respond with greater competence and greater joy in the learning process to the trainee trainer or supervisor's expectation that they will naturally want to learn, grow and develop, rather than to an undue anticipation of 'resistance' on their part by the trainer. In our view resistance is a term frequently misused to describe a multitude of potentially interruptive or restrictive factors in the learning process which range from natural plateaux on the learning curve to the external manifestations of archaic unresolved fears. When trainee trainers or supervisors are experienced as 'resistant', in the first place we look to how their teachers or supervisors may be initiating, contributing to or not resolving their part of the responsibility for the problems.

If it is assumed that human beings have a basic drive for effectiveness, competence and excellence (and are not *solely* envious, destructive or resistant to learning) it becomes easier to see that if trainees are not learning there is possibly another kind of problem. For example, they may have been educationally traumatized, or there may be a learner–teacher mismatch, or they may be studying for a profession or approach for which they are not suited. In the last instance, they may be better off stopping, delaying or changing their training.

*Respect for individual differences*
The next core concept which guides our work is a thorough validation of individual differences. Each human being is unique and the range of needs in counselling, supervision and training is so varied that it is vital for trainee supervisors and trainers to cultivate an attitude of delight in difference. The trainers of counsellor trainers and supervisors need to convey this congruently and respectfully to their trainees in order for this growth-enhancing culture to be carried through in the eventual training and supervision of their trainees. Individual learning styles are honoured in so far as they can interact productively with common goals of personal development, theoretical understanding, clinical competence and professional responsibility.

We encourage freedom of thought, excitement in exploration, emphasis on individuality and a reluctance to accept a single doctrine or one standardized way as an ultimate truth. It is essential to find the particular strengths and development areas of each unique person and to design supervisory structures and training programmes which combine the widest possible respect for individual difference with the preservation of shared high standards. Teaching works best if it is geared to 'who the person is'. Respect for the personal learning 'fingerprint' demonstrates overtly the underlying ethos of expecting everyone to take responsibility for realizing their own way of being supervisors and trainers and in their turn to pass it on.

One of the many ways in which we believe this appreciation of individuality and difference is modelled within a training institution or a supervisory structure is through the availability of multiple role models. Trainee trainers and supervisors benefit from having at least one long-standing supervisory relationship with someone who can guide their long-term development. In addition, the availability of several other supervisors provides a range of models to enhance individual learning. Trainee trainers and supervisors can in this process experience that competence and excellence may come in a variety of very different, and sometimes even contradictory, packages.

### The concept of individual responsibility

At the heart of this orientation in the training of trainee trainers and supervisors is the concept of individual responsibility for one's own behaviour (whether conscious or unconscious) *as well as* responsibility towards others. While excellence is sought in terms of individual development it has to find its realization within a framework of respect for others. People are deemed responsible for their own learning processes and this includes responsibility for getting the best from their own trainers and supervisors.

We have found it important to develop and challenge the learning community so that it inevitably has to deal with the inherent paradox between the values of co-operation and individuality and also between a demand for competence and an acceptance of the human individual right to unique identity.

### Congruence

An important aspect in the training of the trainers of counsellors and supervisors is the development of core principles of learning and education which are congruent with the philosophy or the value system underlying the material which is to be taught. All trainees are alert to the difference between 'the way you walk and the way you talk'. Incongruity or inauthenticity between the manner of teaching and its content will undermine the effectiveness of training or supervision. *What* is being taught or conveyed (content) must match *how* it is conveyed (process). In the training of trainers and supervisors, it is essential that the people are suitable for the work *and* that their performance meets certain standards of competence. There is a difference between 'being' and 'doing'. A good person or a good clinician is not necessarily the same as a good supervisor or a good trainer. The development of specialist skills needs to be encouraged as well as the development of integrative skills for effective training or supervision.

*Willingness to change and respect for tradition*
We have found that trainees at all levels enjoy contributing to the setting of standards to develop excellence in their field of work. A commitment to the status quo and a reluctance to improve, grow, develop or change is antithetical to the very nature of counselling and the learning process. Trainee trainers and supervisors who need this kind of 'security' are probably in the wrong line of work. Obviously the emphasis on excellence and development needs to be balanced with the demands of time, comparability with other trainings and the inherent fallibility of human achievement against perfectionistic ideals. It is unwise to make the unrealistic 'better' the enemy of the 'good'. However, it is also important to encourage improving judgement and developing quality which is independent of unconditional acceptance of the individual person. Failing a person in an accrediting procedure or discouraging them from continuing to train or supervise must not imply a rejection of personal value (even though it may briefly feel that way at the time).

Self-discovery, learning by personal experience and self-direction is vital, and yet it is important to be aware of the continuing generations of thinkers and workers who have been so active this century, and probably since the beginning of time, in addressing themselves to furthering the course of human self-understanding and the alleviation of suffering. We stand on the shoulders of the people who went before us.

## The process of training trainers and supervisors in terms of a natural learning cycle

*Supervisor training*
New supervisors tend to supervise in the manner in which they have

previously been supervised. Training in supervision therefore involves some unlearning of earlier introjected styles, and the development of the person's own individual style of supervision. It is generally held that supervision needs to be conducted in the manner of the counselling system in which the counsellor is working. However, many counselling supervisors now employ an integrative approach to supervision which subsumes a variety of approaches and techniques.

### Trainer training

Training is defined as bringing a person '. . . to [a] desired state or standard of efficiency etc. by instruction and practice' (McKintosh, 1961: 1354). Of course in training trainers, the very process of instruction and practice by which we instruct the trainees becomes the pattern or blueprint for teaching. Any individualized training plan must be designed to fit the temperament, learning needs and thinking style of the person while seeking also to redress any particular educational deficit or trauma suffered by the person. Experiences of paralysing anxiety or 'stage-fright' before leading a training or supervision session, prolonged lack of confidence, exhaustion or strain after apparently successful trainings or supervision, and persistent beliefs that 'this success was only a fluke' and 'I continue to believe that I'm a fraud and that my trainees, supervisees or colleagues or examining boards will find out that I don't really know what I'm doing' signal the pseudo-competency syndrome referred to earlier.

In our experience, many people who train as trainers or supervisors have experienced, and so carry the scars of, previous academic trauma. This necessitates careful nurturing of dormant curiosity and incipient creativity as well as patience and delicacy. Trainee trainers and supervisors often require counselling themselves to deal with the long-term debilitating or inhibiting effects of previously neglectful or destructive teaching or supervision. Skill and experience in helping trainee trainers and supervisors with such discrepancies or interruptions of their natural learning cycles build competence as well as confidence and encourage self-esteem and courage.

In the process of training and supervising a large number of counselling trainers and supervisors, we have often observed a difference between the training needs, skills and developmentally appropriate learning of trainers at the beginning, intermediate or the advanced stages. We see these three stages as roughly corresponding to three phases on the learning cycle – from unconscious incompetence to conscious incompetence; from conscious incompetence to conscious competence; and from conscious competence to unconscious competence. (This is a schema we adapted from Robinson, 1974.) We have named these three phases Awareness, Accommodation and Assimilation. We do not conceptualize these stages as clearly demarcated, but more as general signposts which mark the supervisor's or trainer's progress from the beginning to the more advanced stages of their own training and development and thus provide some check-list for what may be needed on each part of the journey. Furthermore we do not think that 'training' ever *ends*: we see it as a lifelong, continuing, cyclic process, whether for counsellors, trainers or supervisors. In the discussion which follows, readers are advised to substitute trainer for supervisor or vice versa as they proceed with the material, since we see both trainers and supervisors as passing through similar developmental stages.

## 1 Awareness: from unconscious incompetence to conscious incompetence

Awareness is bringing into consciousness the person's sense and identification of what needs to be learnt. This phase concerns the assessment of learning needs and an awareness of gaps, confusion or errors in skills and knowledge. Of course hardly anyone considered for the job of trainer will be completely incompetent. The terminology is meant to highlight the movement from unconsciousness to consciousness in the areas which the trainee has to master. From what has been said before, we know this will best be done against the background of valuing what the trainee has already accomplished and an appreciation of the skills already established. Here the focus is on what still needs to be taught through diagnosis or assessment.

Co-working with more senior trainers gives beginners the opportunity both to receive supervision of their own teaching and to model on an experienced trainer. Many people report that such co-working is a very different experience from being a participant in a training group, since this time they are looking at the group from a trainer's perspective and assessing challenges from this vantage point. This facilitates change in the frame of reference essential for the effective trainer.

At the beginning stage, trainers sometimes appear successful because the group members are *kind* to them, sensing their nervousness and vulnerability. 'We could see how scared you were from the way the paper shook in your hands.' The beginning trainer needs to learn to manage his or her anxiety and develop skills in handling group process. This involves acquiring or refining techniques for dealing with challenging group members and especially having a knowledge of the different stages and effective management procedures of group development (Clarkson, 1988) so that, for example, the *storming phase*, when the group members are testing the group boundaries and the leader's authority, is not experienced as a personal insult or assault. They need to be able to differentiate transferential reactions based on people's previous educational experiences from genuine feedback on their own style. For example, unwillingness to do experiential exercises may be the result of prior mismanaged 'role-playing' techniques or a genuine rejection of the manner in which the beginning trainer has introduced the structure to the training group. The ability to handle group interaction to enhance experimentation, responsibility and learning is acquired both by observation and practice. Seeing another person survive and handle the group process serves as a model for future skills development.

This first phase often appears to be categorized for new supervisors by the unconscious reproduction of the behaviour, attitudes and frames of reference of their own supervisors. This, of course, provides a bridge for passing on effective behaviours and attitudes, but also involves passing on mistakes or blind spots as long as such previous experience remains merely *introjected* instead of *integrated*. As trainee supervisors learn more about supervision through observation and direct teaching, they become conscious of a certain limited number of strategies which they habitually use. At this stage damage limitation is important and beginning supervisors need to be keenly aware of the limits of their own competence. They may need to be told what *not* to do!

Further challenges for the beginning trainer or supervisor involve a shifting balance between content and process, between structure and flexibility, between transmitting accurate information and creativity. For every person the goal is to discover without harsh judgement or undue self-flattery what indeed they have garnered of value in their own experience and knowledge of training and what are the areas of potential development. For trainers the skill lies in maintaining the self-confidence and trust of trainee trainers in the learning process while discovering and tolerating the gaps in their knowledge, skills or competence until confrontation is appropriate.

*2 Accommodation: from conscious incompetence to*
*conscious competence*
In accommodation, the system adapts itself to new material which

may at this stage still be experienced as foreign or different from the self, just like food which is inadequately digested. The trainee trainer or supervisor may take on new ideas and try them out in a mannered or stylized way without necessarily taking into account their relevance to a particular situation or supervisee. Throughout this stage trainee trainers will be adapting themselves to the requirements of the new material and the new teaching situation. To the observer this process may at times appear jerky and unrhythmical as the trainee trainer or supervisor explores how they can accommodate themselves to the raw material, new methods or improved structures.

A frequent challenge at this stage involves learning to deal with 'difficult' people in a group and to acquire strategies for handling defensiveness or anxiety in group members. A trainer needs to learn to use difficult or critical situations to enhance the learning potential for all members in the group. For example, how the trainer deals with a potential scapegoating situation becomes an internal reference point for the future for all participants of a training or supervision group. Trainee trainers may sometimes over- or under-react to challenging group members, as they have not yet developed a firm and secure sense of their own authority as trainers and the new learning they are incorporating does not yet sit comfortably with them.

Trainee supervisors or trainers may become rigid and develop predictable styles of reacting based on what has worked in one situation, rather than varying their interpersonal style and so retaining the element of surprise that maintains interest and involvement. Such a lack of flexibility is the antithesis of creativity and spontaneity. In this phase potential trainers may become disheartened and discouraged by the gap they perceive between themselves and the really experienced, skilled or even gifted trainers or supervisors they have observed or experienced. Support for their strengths and encouragement for their deficiencies is vital from a supervising trainer if they are to continue growing in competence and confidence when motivation may be fluctuating. The challenge for the supervising trainer is to shift between supporting the new supervisor or trainer's existing skills and challenging the person to extend his or her repertoire by acquiring more refined skills. Realistic feedback about the new trainer's strengths and weaknesses is an essential part of this process of self-development. It is important that new trainers realistically assess what they have achieved, as this relates to their *own* level of development, and do not expect to become experienced trainers overnight or make comparisons which hinder rather than help.

This second phase in the training of supervisors is often accompanied by an experience of being 'de-skilled' as their strategic and theoretical horizons widen. Supervisors sometimes report an experience of being 'swamped' in the same way that a prospective novelist may be in wanting to account for every aspect of the situation. There is a need for maps, sorting procedures and for methods of categorization which help identify possible key issues. Observing, selecting and focusing are therefore key skills to develop at this phase. This process of selection is reflected in the more experienced supervisor's mastery of selecting priorities and focusing on key issues in the context of a facilitative supervisory relationship. Respect and genuine positive regard for all learners (regardless of the stage of development) is an essential underpinning for increasing excellence and vitality in the process.

We have found that an emphasis on the contractual nature of supervision has assisted new supervisors to focus on the most relevant area for supervision, rather than taking on so wide a brief that they end up achieving no creative outcome at all with the supervisee. A supervision contract needs to involve a specific statement of what is to be achieved in a particular supervision session or supervisory relationship. This outcome must be behaviourally observable so that its completion can be assessed at the end of the session and all parties can benefit from feedback. Trainers need to learn how to manage both the content of what needs to be conveyed as well as the process of the group within the given time boundaries.

### 3 Assimilation: from conscious competence to unconscious competence

In assimilation the new learning or new skill is absorbed into the system so that it is incorporated and becomes part of the self. Perls et al. (1951) referred to this as 'mental metabolism': whereas before there was some 'self-consciousness' about using newly acquired or rediscovered skills and knowledge, these are now an integral part of the trainer or supervisor. At this stage the challenge is to maintain flexibility and variety in teaching style and in the manner of interaction with group members since habituation may set in.

Important at this advanced stage is the development and refining of the ability to design a learning experience on the spot to meet an existing need in a group member or in the group as a whole. For this the trainer needs a much wider repertoire of skills and the ability to deal with different people at different levels of development in the same training group.

Advanced trainers learn to recognize their own authority and ability and so model excellence and the appreciation of their own worth to their trainees. They also take on the responsibility to train and educate younger, less-experienced trainers through a system of apprenticing, modelling and coaching beginners. Younger people can see experienced trainers as they train. In this way the experienced trainers can get feedback on what they do well so that they can later articulate this to others. This will also prevent experienced trainers from remaining in the area of *unconscious competence* where they are no longer able to identify or pass on their skills. An apprentice often gives far more reliable feedback than can be got from group members, because the apprentice is viewing the process both from the perspective of a trainer and that of a trainee. It is as if they 'see the stitching on the back of the piece of lovely embroidery' and can thus fully appreciate the care and delicacy invested in the finished product.

We consider it vitally important that experienced trainers continue to build new opportunities into their training situation to stretch and extend themselves. By creating ongoing challenges and learning opportunities for themselves they will prevent the staleness that undermines and depletes many previously excellent trainers, leaving them bored and disillusioned with their work or again, unconsciously incompetent as in the beginning of the cycle. Habitual mannerisms and 'hardening of the categories' are possible pitfalls for experienced trainers with their increase in confidence and their unselfconscious skill.

Fine teachers enhance and confirm the worth of all participants ('I feel more intelligent and more gifted when I'm with my trainer') without diminishing their own excellence through false modesty. Problematic teachers elevate themselves at the cost of group members who may end up believing they are inadequate and could never aspire to the 'heights' of the trainer. Experienced supervisors and trainers who have built some reputation benefit from the halo effect – the anticipatory positive expectations that the 'great teacher' will do 'great teaching or supervision'. However they also suffer from the 'pedestal effect' – the frequent human desire to 'find or invent feet of clay' which can preoccupy trainees at the expense of their learning.

Experienced supervisors need to work with a range of supervisees so that they gain experience across a wide spectrum. It is important that they continue to supervise beginning counsellors so that they retain their appreciation of the beginner's process. At the outset of this new stage of training, it may be important for trainee supervisors to relinquish again their previous frame of reference and accustomed ways of approaching problems and tasks in favour of what we call *beginner's mind* – being empty of previous assumptions and set patterns of working. We have personally found it useful at intervals to recreate experientially such conditions by learning new and apparently unrelated skills such as Tai Chi. The more experienced the supervisor, the more important it may be for them to find situations where they 'worry' (again or for the first time) about what 'the teacher' may think of them, where they experience the characteristic jerkiness of the learning process and the excruciating self-consciousness of those first risks and clumsy mistakes as well as the burgeoning sense of achievement in the perhaps small moments of early achievement.

This practice of putting oneself back into the frame of mind of the beginner assists the experienced supervisor to sharpen his or her empathy for the learner. In addition, experienced supervisors continue in supervision, thereby further refining their own skills and extending their empathy for the position of the supervisee. The experienced supervisor needs to guard against complacency and avoid sloppiness and lack of discipline, which may be a temptation for someone who knows their field extremely well. Often, having an apprentice supervisor in sessions who is supervising under supervision, will act as a spur to the experienced supervisor to elucidate clearly and review his or her own style. In Britain the BAC supervisor recognition process for counselling supervisors serves as an excellent challenge for the experienced supervisor to receive reliable and useful feedback about his or her supervisory skills and style.

From what has been said here, it must be clear that the learning cycle never ends. There can hardly be a final product or an accomplished steady state in a discipline such as counselling which continues to evolve and which demands of its practitioners continued flexibility and willingness to keep developing. As soon as one cycle is completed, another one begins. In our view this is natural. It is not a compulsive, externally motivated search for mystical perfection, it is more a natural organismic urge to grow and develop and to become more skilled, more understanding and more compassionate. Being in touch with this evolutionary drive in ourselves enables trainers of trainers and supervisors to experience, model and inspire their charges in similar ways.

### The content of supervisor and trainer training

The principles of adult education and learning theory can be an asset to any trainee trainer and supervisor, particularly if they are willing to blend their own individuality with received wisdom and scientific findings. Trainee trainers are often expected to start training simply because they know a subject without any special *training* in training at all. The first challenge for the trainer of trainers is the weeding out of bad habits carried over from past experiences, for example interminable lecturing without regard for scientific research on optimal concentration spans. Indeed, a lecturer has been known to talk for an hour-and-a-half on the fact that the human concentration span is no longer than 20 minutes! Many a long, monotonous lecture has also been given on the importance of experiential learning. A knowledge of learning theory – how people learn – provides useful information to buttress the skills required to create a good learning environment in which people can benefit with maximum efficiency and pleasure from what the trainer has to offer.

Obviously, a sound knowledge of the subject matter is a basic prerequisite to most effective training and supervision. Any trainer requires a firm grasp of the material, sufficient experience to provide a fertile source for examples and an ongoing sensitivity to the vicissitudes of practice. Supervising clinicians who remain in the field working with the ongoing challenges of their practice are usually experienced as having greater authority and authenticity as teachers than supervisors who are no longer active in clinical practice. The assumption is frequently made that anyone who has been taught can therefore automatically teach. However, as we have pointed out, experience may make an expert but not necessarily an expert teacher. For this reason among others, the training of trainers is an even more neglected area than the training of supervisors. Several areas of competence will need to be acquired by the prospective trainer and supervisor. No doubt there are many more, but we have isolated those which seem to be most conspicuous when they are lacking.

An extensive discussion of all the important topics essential to supervisor and trainer training is obviously well beyond the scope of this chapter. Space permits only a brief comment on the identified themes (along with a few selected examples) which have proved most useful over many years of training supervisors and trainers in fields ranging from psychodynamic psychotherapy to clinical psychology, and from person-centred or gestalt approaches to counselling and psychotherapy to individual, group or organizational contexts. Those topics can be addressed in the form of an established syllabus, as in the metanoia Psychotherapy Institute's supervision course, from which most of this material has been drawn, or by means of several modules put together over a varying period of time in a number of different combinations of structures and/or self-study:

- The nature and varieties of relationship
- The importance and use of individual learning styles
- Contracts and contracting
- Conceptual models
- Educational methods, means and media
- Intervention strategies and techniques
- Transference, countertransference and parallel process in supervision
- Selecting priorities and sequences
- Values and ethics
- Organizational or contextual factors
- Group dynamics, group development and group management: methods and goals
- Developmental stages of learning
- Timing and rhythm
- Evaluation of process and outcome
- Special preparation for examination or assessment procedures
- Self-care and modelling of personal and professional development
- The relationship between student and teacher or trainer and training group

### The nature and varieties of relationship

Trainee trainers and supervisors will raise issues in training and supervision that require different kinds or styles of relationship on the part of the trainer (Clarkson, 1990a). Of central importance in any successful learning process is *the working alliance* between the supervisor or trainer and the trainee. The working alliance is an Adult-to-Adult agreement between the trainee and trainer which marks the trainee's willingness to engage in a learning relationship, even at times when at some archaic level they may not wish to do so. Such a working alliance forms the basis of a mutually satisfactory trainer–trainee educational experience. In our experience this working alliance is based on mutual respect and an understanding of individual needs and differences.

Another type of relationship that is important in training and supervising is *the I–Thou relationship* (Buber, 1970). This is often referred to as the real relationship or the core relationship and involves an authentic encounter between two people. In the training and supervisory process the I–Thou relationship is characterized by the here-and-now existential encounter between the two people. It involves mutual participation in the learning process and the recognition that each is changed by this interaction. Personal self-disclosure on the part of the supervisor/trainer will, if sparingly used, facilitate the process of trainee learning. If trainers or supervisors admit to their own fallibility and vulnerability at appropriate moments, this will help the trainee trainers and supervisors to appreciate the common humanity that joins them. In our experience, this relationship is a powerful factor in helping trainees to develop self-esteem and self-respect.

In any training or supervisory setting, *the transferential relationship* will need to be taken into account. In the transference, infantile prototypes re-emerge and are experienced with a strong sensation of immediacy. In the training and supervisory process, the transference evoked by the teaching situation often triggers the trainee back to unsatisfactory classroom situations and experiences from their past learning contexts. The trainer/supervisor needs to be alert to the high likelihood that the trainee will be unconsciously experiencing them as they did their teachers in childhood. Resolving such transferences requires active steps on the part of the trainer to establish a healthy learning environment in which respect for the individual is coupled with creative teaching and caring confrontation. Unhealthy countertransference (both negative and positive) on the part of trainee trainers and supervisors, both in response to their trainers/supervisors or their own trainees and supervisees, needs to be dealt with in personal counselling or enabled in supervision (Clarkson, 1990b).

Another type of relationship of central importance in training is the *developmentally needed relationship*. This is the intentional provision by the trainer of a corrective/reparative or replenishing parental (or teacher) relationship in cases where the original parenting (teaching) was deficient, abusive or over-protective. In our experience, the trainer/supervisor frequently needs to fill the developmental gaps which resulted from earlier inadequate learning experiences. Many trainees who manifest thinking problems in adulthood were subject to educational trauma combined with an inadequate response on the part of their teachers or parents to what was developmentally appropriate for them.

### The importance and use of individual learning styles
There is a distinction between style and competence. Style is the idiosyncratic articulation of individual competence and will be unique to each individual. We know that learning is more effective if people retain and develop their individual styles. Trainers of

counsellor trainers and supervisors will therefore be dealing with a wide range of individual differences which need to be respected and fostered. Making many exceptions often leads to exceptional results. Some of these differences will concern temperament (for example introversion/extroversion), pacing of learning, academic ability, cultural variables or a preference for learning experientially or primarily through visual or auditory channels (Bandler and Grinder, 1975, 1976). All of these need to be taken into account practically, in terms of designing learning experiences and structures, as well as philosophically, in terms of cherishing individuality.

There are many maps or grids available for exploring and understanding differences in learning styles. It is important that the supervisor be aware of and comfortably use at least some of these. For example, Kolb et al. (1984) differentiate between accommodators, divergers, convergers and assimilators, depending on their relative position on the two axes, concrete experience to abstract conceptualization and active experimentation to reflective observation. An accommodator's strength lies in doing things, in carrying out plans and tasks where the chief need is to adapt oneself to changing immediate circumstances. The diverger is imaginative and able to view concrete situations from many perspectives and organize these into a meaningful whole. The converger's greatest strength lies in problem solving, decision making and the practical application of ideas. An assimilator's greatest strength lies in inductive reasoning and in the ability to assimilate observations into an integrated theoretical model. Another model of learning styles developed by Peter Honey and Alan Mumford (1989) describes four types of learning style preferences. They are '. . . Activist: I'll try anything once. Reflector: I'd like time to think about this. Theorist: How does this fit with that? Pragmatist: How can I apply this in practice?' The aim for the trainee trainer would be to capitalize on strengths and acquire the other capacities so that all four styles can be comfortably accommodated within his or her repertoire.

*Contracts and contracting*

A contract may be defined as a mutual commitment to achieving a specific set of goals and outcomes from the training/supervision process. A contract is worded in behaviourally specific language so that both parties are quite clear when the stated goal has been achieved. Learning to make appropriate contracts, meeting the contract through well-chosen interventions and knowing when to change a contract are important skills to be learnt by new trainers and supervisors. A contract, by clearly specifying what both parties are going to deliver and expect to receive, avoids disappointment and confused communication. The trainee trainer/supervisor will also learn to focus his or her energies appropriately on a relevant goal with the aid of the contracting process. For each specific supervision session it is generally advisable that the trainee supervisor and supervisee have a well-defined contract. Trainee supervisors and supervisees may also make longer-term supervisory contracts for, say, a period of a year at a time, which specify the supervisee's learning goals for that period.

*Conceptual models*
Supervision and training practice is improved if supported and underlined by sound conceptual models, effective tools and helpful maps. Even though people may choose to work from different conceptual models, we believe that it is important to review theoretically and at regular intervals what is being done and to change models in response to changing needs and situations. We employ an integrative model of training and supervision with an emphasis on including findings from various approaches to supervision and training rather than on a single view of the training/ supervision process. A comprehensive model is coherent and takes into account research evidence and insights from different approaches. We consider it important that supervisors and trainers be familiar with a variety of conceptual models, since they may be severely limited if they are confined to their own model or a single psychological language. On the other hand if expertise is to be developed in a specialized area, a specialist approach may be indicated.

Supervision training needs to be supplemented by plentiful practice of supervision, supervised supervision and 'cascade' supervision (here a counsellor is supervised by a supervisor who is in turn supervised by the supervising trainer). Supervision can be done live or with the use of audio, video or by case consultation. Trainee trainers can practise samples of teaching for longer or shorter periods, for example ten to fifteen minute segments. They can also practise group management skills and answering questions, as well as developing longer-term skills such as course design and syllabus planning.

*Educational methods, means and media*
There appears to be a correlation between the richness and variety of teaching means and methods and the depth or efficiency of learning. The range of teaching aids – questionnaires, films, video-playback, 'family sculpts' with buttons (creating a model of family relationships using buttons), experiential exercises, the use of

playdough and the employment of a large Lego set (to use for demonstrating group dynamics in team-building exercises) – is vast, stimulating and limited only by the imagination of the trainer or supervisor.

The fertile interplay between right-hemispheric and left-hemispheric learning can be facilitated by using creative media. For example a trainee trainer used a hot-water bottle, a clump of grass, a piece of carpet, a milk bottle and an Israeli song to consolidate her learning about the interplay of prediction and intuition in treatment design (Clarkson, 1991).

*Intervention strategies and techniques*
It is recommended that a trainee trainer work out in advance an overall strategy and training plan in which the separate segments of the material to be covered are sequentially and developmentally arranged. Trainee supervisors can learn to adapt their strategies (whether pre-planned or spontaneous) depending on the circumstances and the needs of the individual. For example, the supervision of trainees on an institutional programme is different from consultation/supervision with very experienced, qualified colleagues. Specific supervisory or teaching techniques may be involved in the actual transmission process. Trainee trainers and supervisors are encouraged to develop a wide range of intervention strategies, not only within their own discipline but also in different learning structures. This may involve variety of style, structure, medium and modality, incorporating some right-hemispheric principles like action learning and accelerated learning, as well as experiential learning. Trainee trainers are encouraged to widen their repertoire beyond their personal preferences, comfort zones, individual inclinations and their own personal histories of being trained. In their training or supervision, it is helpful to have knowledge of, and take into account, transference issues and relationships to authority as these manifest in the training context. Such an approach leads directly to creating individualized training plans, rather than submitting all trainee trainers and supervisors to an identical process.

*Transference, countertransference and parallel process*
Both the trainee trainer and supervisor require a knowledge of how transference, countertransference and parallel process may be operative in the educational process. An understanding of parallel process can be obtained by analysing the interaction between transferential and countertransferential relationships as these are reflected in a training group or in the supervisory relationship.

Effective trainee supervisors need to be particularly alert to the potential parallel process between the supervisor–supervisee relationship and the relationship with a client that the supervisee is bringing to supervision. Frequently a counselling supervisee will enact in the supervision session the very problem that he or she is experiencing with a client. The trainee supervisor will gradually acquire the skill to prevent duplicating the problem in the supervision process with the counsellor. (See also Chapter 6, pp. 92–3.)

*Selecting priorities and sequences*

A challenge for the trainee supervisor is the selection of priorities or key issues in a supervision session, as well as selecting priorities at different stages of trainee development. In training supervisors we have found it useful to think of different bands or categories of key issues which help trainee supervisors to sort out the apparently overwhelming mass of competing details, impressions and responses so characteristic of the supervisory process. We shall discuss briefly here *the bands of supervision* (Clarkson and Gilbert, 1990). These bands or categories provide the trainee supervisor with a series of five broad categories, each of which could be the focus in a particular supervision session. The trainee supervisor selects from amongst the bands that band (or bands) which he or she considers to be the priority in a particular session. The trainee supervisor often experiences difficulty in sorting out priorities and these bands of supervision have proved helpful in choosing a focus. In any given supervision session, the trainee supervisor may work in two or at the most three of the bands, having selected these in terms of the supervisee's needs.

1  *Assessment and treatment planning – how to think about the situation*: Most practitioners use some method of assessing client problems, strengths and weaknesses. Assessment may be very formal (for example, the use of a diagnostic system like the DSM-III-R) or less formal, and describe the client's dynamics and presenting problems in the language appropriate to the particular counselling approach. For many counsellors, accurate assessment is intimately related to effective short- and long-term treatment planning or treatment design. The focus in this band is on stages of treatment and the choice of techniques appropriate to the client at a particular stage of treatment. A counsellor may, for example, lack an awareness of overall treatment goals while focusing too narrowly on a particular aspect of the client's functioning.

2  *Strategies and intervention techniques – what can be done in the*

*situation*: Training in particular treatment strategies and therapeutic techniques forms the focus in this band of supervision. A
counsellor may, for example, be using the same technique or
intervention strategy again and again because of the lack of a
wider repertoire of choices and options in his or her therapeutic
'tool kit'. The particular therapeutic techniques focused upon
will relate to the counselling approach used by the counsellor
coming for supervision, whether this be person-centred counselling, Transactional Analysis counselling or psychodynamic
counselling.

3   *Parallel process (reflection of transference/countertransference
    dynamic) – interferences or facilitation in the situation*: The
    beginning counsellor in particular seems prone to focus on those
    problems in the client that highlight the counsellor's own diffi-
    culties in learning, which may be reflected in the supervisory
    relationship. Certain difficulties in the counselling relationship
    may be due to the trainee's own unresolved issues from the past
    which are interfering with the smooth flow of counselling. An
    identification of such issues and a commitment to resolve these
    in personal counselling will be an important goal for the
    developing counsellor. Countertransference reactions, if clearly
    understood as such, can be used to gain insights which can prove
    to be useful in helping the client.

4   *Theory (teaching and integration) – explanations of the situation*:
    Providing theoretical information forms an essential part of
    training and supervision. Training of course provides one of the
    primary modes in which the trainee gains information.
    However, one of the purposes of supervision is to assist the
    supervisee to integrate theoretical learning from their past or
    current training into their client practice. Supervision provides
    an ongoing forum for the integration of such learning into
    practice.

5   *Ethics and professional practice – values in the situation*: This
    supervision 'band' embraces issues of professional practice and
    ethics as these relate to the trainee counsellor in his or her
    relationships with clients and with professional peers. A spec-
    trum of problems, ranging from confidentiality with clients and
    how to deal with advertising practice, to difficulties in dealing
    with a professional colleague, may take priority here as the focus
    of supervision.

We have found that these bands of key issues and priorities in
supervision are also useful for the trainee trainer. They provide
both trainee trainer and supervisor with a helpful tool for focusing

their attention and concentration in a particular session. The criteria for the selection of a particular band will involve considerations like the developmental level of the trainee, areas which may be consistently avoided by a trainee, and the priority given to critical issues (such as suicide) over any other material that has been presented.

*Values and ethics*
In this section it is essential to study the codes of ethics for supervisors and trainers as these have been developed by different organizations, notably by the British Association for Counselling (see Appendix). Trainees, at whatever level, need to be aware of the privileges and the limitations of their profession. In training both trainers and supervisors in the knowledge and practice of values and ethical principles, we have found an experiential approach to be the most valuable. It is important that trainee trainers and supervisors realize the difference between principles and laws. Principles need to be thought about and applied with care, sensitivity and intelligence in the relevant situation. Beginning counsellors have often expressed anxiety that there is no absolute law governing values and ethics. They need to be taught through discussion and experiential exercises that what is crucial in dealing with ethical and professional issues is the ability to think ethically and to work back to basic principles while applying these in a humane manner. This is best done by trainee trainers who have themselves been through the same process with the appropriate code of ethics.

In summary, beginning counsellors need not only to know the concrete principles but also to develop the *process* of thinking about ethics. It is important that the trainee trainer/supervisor contextualize counselling trainees within the social and political system in which they are practising.

*Organizational or contextual factors*
In a systems model of supervision or training, the trainer takes into account the various people and agencies that may be influencing both the client and the supervisee. We take account of the many contexts in which people operate and which need to be accounted for in an assessment of the client's current situation. In Figure 10.1 we demonstrate our systems framework. The client is in a direct relationship with the worker/counsellor with whom the client has a counselling relationship. The supervisor has a direct relationship with the counsellor, which by its very nature involves an indirect relationship with the client. If supervision is taking place in an agency setting or if the counsellor works in an agency, then the

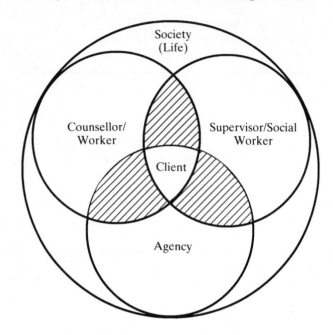

Figure 10.1 *The training/supervisory system*

supervisor has either a direct or indirect relationship with that agency. Each delineated area overlaps with others, which helps in focusing on a different segment of the system. We have encircled this whole process to indicate that it takes place in the context of society as a whole. This systems model is an aid to the supervisor for whom the multifaceted context in which the supervisor and supervisee operate is an important factor in the supervision process.

*Group dynamics, group development and group management: methods and goals*
Sensitive and effective management of group process can rest on a purely intuitive grasp and on 'playing it by ear', particularly if the ear is highly skilled. In training beginning trainers, a specific knowledge of group process and of the stages of group development is usually experienced as supportive and it has been described as one of the single most helpful areas of information for beginning trainers whether in education, management or counsellor training. Personal experience of group dynamics, its unfolding and the factors that can hinder or facilitate the establishment of high-performing groups are best forged on the anvil of subjective exper-

ience informed by the best that current science can offer. Skills must range from the specifics of teaching feedback skills to the subtleties of establishing and maintaining a trusting environment.

## Developmental stages of learning

It is essential that trainers and supervisors use a model of developmental stages within the learning process. Many such models have been documented (Fleming, 1953; Hogan, 1964; Stoltenberg and Delworth, 1987: Wiley, 1982).

These models describe in different terms the stages through which a trainee counsellor passes in the course of his or her development as a counsellor. Many of these models describe a move from dependency on the supervisor when the counsellor tends to be insecure and lacking in confidence, to a middle stage in which the counsellor develops his or her knowledge and skills and deals with personal issues that influence the counselling context, and then to a final stage in which the counsellor is more independent of the supervisor and has begun to develop his or her own individual style of counselling. Trainee counsellors require different types of input at these different developmental stages.

We have used our own model of developmental stages in the development of trainee trainers and supervisors in writing this chapter. This model reflects both changes across time and inherent patterns of development that occur in the training process. In our model we have outlined three stages which we have called Awareness, Accommodation and Assimilation, as discussed in detail on pp. 149–54.

## Timing and rhythm

An intervention given at the right time can immeasurably enhance its value. An effective trainee trainer/supervisor must develop patience to wait until the trainee counsellor is ready to learn something new as part of a natural process. There is a season to people taking in new material or changing their frame of reference and the good trainer will wait for the trainee counsellor's interest and readiness to ripen.

Time management is a vital part of good training and supervision. The trainer needs to tailor his or her material to the time available, whether this be a session, a day or a year's training plan. The trainee trainer/supervisor will also be modelling for the trainee counsellor the importance of time as a boundary in the learning process.

## Evaluation of process and outcome

There are a number of criteria that we consider important in the evaluation of process and outcome in training and supervision. As mentioned above, clear *contracts* made at the beginning of a session are an important part of the training process. The trainee trainer/ supervisor can then assess at the end of the process whether the contract has been met satisfactorily. Another criterion for evaluation is whether the *key concepts* relating to the material have been conveyed to the counselling trainee. These key concepts will be outlined in the syllabus which guides the trainee trainer. For the trainee supervisor we have given a list of key issues under bands of supervision in the section 'Selecting priorities and sequences' above (pp. 161–3). Evaluation of supervision involves an assessment of whether the trainee supervisor has identified such key issues in the supervisory process. A further criterion for evaluating process is to assess whether the trainee supervisor/trainer has performed in a congruent *manner*. Does the medium match the message? *Damage limitation* (taking effective action to ensure that a trainee counsellor is not behaving in a manner that may harm his or her clients) is another important factor in evaluating the effectiveness of training and supervision. Has the trainee trainer/supervisor considered how trainees might abuse the material and taken reasonable precautions to avoid such abuse? Finally, in evaluating successful training and supervision the assessor will take into account whether the trainee trainer/supervisor has maintained *a respectful relationship* towards trainees.

*Special preparation for examination or assessment procedures*

The development of competence is a natural organismic process which will differ for each individual in the course of their training. In an effective training programme self-, peer and tutor assessment all play their part. Assessment of competence is not necessarily the same as preparing people to take a particular examination. Trainee counsellors need to be aware of the criteria for competence in counselling so that they can measure themselves against these as they progress through their training.

In preparing trainees to take examinations, we put the stress on caring for the people who are going forward for examination. It is of course important that trainees be able to take the stress of an examination. This also prepares and tests them for dealing with the stress of client relationships since practising counsellors need in the course of their work to be able to withstand higher levels of stress from their clients than they are ever likely to experience in assessments or examinations.

*Self-care and modelling of personal and professional
development*

Trainers and supervisors need to attend to the area of their personal skills and development in an ongoing way. This includes the trainer's personal counselling or psychotherapy needs, presentation of self, quality of relationships and the quality of their life-style. The general quality of a trainer's life-style needs to support the demanding profession of counselling, training and supervising. For people working in this demanding profession, regular contact with family, friends and peers, as well as the back-up of continuing training, supervision and personal-growth opportunities, are essential for replenishing reserves. Counsellors must take care to get sufficient personal satisfaction outside of their counselling work and be aware of the dangers of 'burnout'. There is growing concern in the literature and the professions about the prevalence of the burnout syndrome among caring workers, since it leads to temporary or permanent incapacitation, for example exhaustion, loss of creativity and enthusiasm for the work, drug dependency (particularly caffeine, nicotine and alcohol), depression, somatic symptoms and perhaps even death through, for example, heart attacks.

*The relationship between student and teacher or trainer and
training group*

An informal survey of important factors in training has revealed the primary importance of the trainer's ability to inspire the learners. Even teachers and trainers who were deficient in most technical skills and who could yet inspire their charges were valued highly despite their other shortcomings. A good teacher can convey a love for and enthusiasm about a subject which remains as a source of motivation for excellence long after the content of what they taught has been forgotten. This usually comprises an ability to pace, prioritize, entertain and involve, as well as an ongoing personal commitment to the subject. The aims of the good trainer are to generate interest, nurture curiosity and guide preferences or individual inclinations in the most fruitful directions. An effective teacher is committed to maximizing the match between the course content and people's individual interests, preferences and motivations.

## Continuing education

For experienced counselling supervisors it is vital to continue to seek situations for personal, professional and educational development. Such continuing education will involve knowledge of new theory in supervision, refinement of skills and a familiarity with supervision research findings and procedures. Supervisors can keep up to date by participating in research, conferences and professional working parties. In addition, listening to their own supervision tapes and having peers sit in on this process will help trainee supervisors to assess their own strengths and growth needs and encourage the humility which is the hallmark of a competent supervisor. It is important for experienced supervisors to pass on their knowledge in an effective manner through writing, running workshops, conducting courses and remaining active in the field of counselling supervision.

Similarly for the trainer, continuing education is vital. Specialist skills need to be acquired, alongside the development of integrative skills. A trainer needs to keep abreast of developments in the particular field of counselling in which they are training, as well as keeping informed about developments in the counselling field. Mostly, it is important to keep the instrument – the 'self' of the trainer or supervisor – in good form and to set an example of self-care by a good quality of life, relationship and recreation as well as continuing professional enhancement. It is by doing this that burnout can be avoided and the evolution of the profession of counselling be most truly aided. At the most fundamental level, in this way we as trainers, supervisors and counsellors can help ensure a better quality of service to the people who turn to us in need.

## References

Aristotle (1970) *Physics* Bks I & II (trans. by W. Charlton). Oxford: Clarendon Press.

Bandler, R. and Grinder, J. (1975) *The Structure of Magic*, I. Palo Alto, Calif.: Science and Behavior Books.

Bandler, R. and Grinder, J. (1976) *The Structure of Magic*, II. Palo Alto, Calif.: Science and Behavior Books.

Buber, M. (1970) *I and Thou* (trans. by W. Kaufmann). Edinburgh: T & T Clark (first published in 1937).

Clarkson, P. (1988) 'Group imago and the stages of group development', *ITA News*, 20: 4–16.

Clarkson, P. (1990a) 'A multiplicity of psychotherapeutic relationships' (accepted for publication in the *British Journal of Psychotherapy*, London).

Clarkson, P. (1990b) 'Transference, countertransference and parallel process in TA' (accepted for publication in the *Transactional Analysis Journal*, San Francisco).

Clarkson, P. (1991) *Transactional Analysis Psychotherapy: An Integrated Approach*. London: Routledge.

Clarkson, P. and Gilbert, M. (1990) *Supervisory Tools* (unpublished manuscript).

Fleming, J. (1953) 'The role of supervision in psychiatric training', *Bulletin of the Menninger Clinic*, 17: 157–9.

Hogan, R.A. (1964) 'Issues and approaches in supervision', *Psychotherapy: Theory, Research and Practice*, 1: 139–41.

Honey, P. and Mumford, A. (1989) 'Trials and tribulations', *Education Guardian*, 19 December: 19.

Kolb, D.A., Rubin, I.M. and McIntyre, J.M. (eds) (1984) *Organizational Psychology*. Englewood Cliffs, NJ: Prentice-Hall.

McKintosh, E. (revised by) (1961) *The Concise Oxford Dictionary*. London: Oxford University Press.

Perls, F.S., Hefferline, R.F. and Goodman, P. (1951/1969) *Gestalt Therapy: Excitement and Growth in the Human Personality*. New York: Julian Press.

Robinson, W.L. (1974) 'Conscious competency – the mark of a competent instructor', *Personnel Journal*, 53: 538–9.

Rosenthal, R. and Jacobson, L. (1968) *Pygmalion in the Classroom: Teacher Expectation and Pupil's Intellectual Development*. New York: Holt, Rinehart & Winston.

Stoltenberg, C.D. and Delworth, U. (1987) *Supervising Counselors and Therapists: A Developmental Approach*. London: Jossey-Bass.

Wiley, M. O'L. (August, 1982) 'Developmental counseling supervision: person–environment congruency, satisfaction and learning', paper presented at the annual meeting of the American Psychological Association, Washington, DC.

# APPENDICES

# BAC Code of Ethics and Practice for Trainers

## A. Code of ethics: trainers

*Introduction*
*The purpose of this Code of Ethics is to establish and maintain standards for trainers and to inform and protect members of the public seeking counselling training.*
*This document should be seen in relation to the Code of Ethics and Practice for Counsellors.*
*Ethical standards comprise such values as integrity, competence, confidentiality and responsibility. Members of this Association, in assenting to this Code, accept their responsibilities to trainees, colleagues and clients, this Association, their agencies and society. Trainers are those who train people to become counsellors or who train people in counselling skills.*
*Trainers endeavour to ensure that when trainees complete the programme of training, the trainees are competent to serve the best interest of the client.*
*The relationship between trainers and trainees is similar in some respects to that between counsellors and clients. Trainees, during some of this training, may find themselves in a vulnerable situation with regard to a trainer where painful and potentially damaging material may be revealed which needs to be handled in a sensitive and caring manner.*
*In other respects, the relationship is different. Trainees are adult learners who bring to the training their prior experience and personal style. This should be respected by trainers and only challenged in relation to the stated objectives of the particular training.*
*Trainers need to be guided by this ethical code so that they can maintain the highest standards of responsibility towards trainees. Therefore this Code of Ethics is a framework within which to work – more a set of instruments than a set of instructions.*

### 1. Issues of Responsibility
### 2. Issues of Competence

*1. Issues of responsibility*
1.1. Training a person as a counsellor in counselling skills is a deliberately undertaken responsibility.

1.2.  Trainers are responsible for the observance of the principles embodied in this Code of Ethics and Practice for Trainers and the Code of Ethics for Counsellors.

1.3.  Trainers must recognise the value and dignity of trainees irrespective of origin, status, sex, sexual orientation, age, belief or contribution to society.

1.4.  Trainers accept a responsibility to encourage and facilitate the self-development of trainees whilst also establishing clear working agreements which indicate the responsibility of trainees for their own continued learning and self-monitoring.

1.5.  Trainers are responsible for setting and monitoring the boundaries between working relationships and friendships or other relationships, and for making boundaries between therapy, consultancy, supervision and training explicit to trainees.

1.6.  Trainers are responsible for ensuring that the satisfaction of their own emotional needs is not dependent upon relationships with their trainees.

1.7.  Trainers should not engage in sexual activity with their trainees whilst also engaging in a training relationship.

1.8.  Trainers should not accept their own trainees for treatment or individual therapy for personal or sexual difficulties should these arise or be revealed during the programme of training. Trainees should be referred to an appropriate individual or agency.

2.  *Issues of Competence*

2.1.  Trainers, having undertaken a basic course in counselling training, should commit themselves to undertake further training as trainers at regular intervals thereafter and consistently seek ways of increasing their professional development and self-awareness.

2.2.  Trainers must monitor their training work and be able to account to trainees and colleagues for what they do and why.

2.3.  Trainers should monitor the limits of their competence.

2.4.  Trainers have a responsibility to themselves and to their trainees to maintain their own effectiveness, resilience, and ability to help trainees, and to know when their personal resources are so depleted as to make it necessary for them to seek help and/or withdraw from counselling training whether temporarily or permanently.

**B.  Code of practice: trainers**

*Introduction:*
*This Code of Practice is intended to provide more specific information and guidance regarding the implementation of the principles embodied in the Code of Ethics for Trainers.*

*1.  Management of the training work:*

1.1.  Trainers should inform trainees as appropriate about their own training, philosophy and theoretical approach, qualifications, and the methods they use.

1.2.  Trainers should be explicit regarding the training programmes and courses offered and what is involved. It is desirable that there should be some consistency between the theoretical orientation of the course and the teaching methods used on it e.g. client-centred courses will tend to be trainee-centred.

1.3.  Any fees required should be disclosed before courses begin.

1.4.  Trainers should be open with intending trainees regarding potential suitability for training and make clear what selection procedures are involved.

1.5.  Trainers have a responsibility to confirm with trainees what therapeutic or helping relationships are in existence before the course begins, and enable trainees to consider their own needs for personal therapy outside the course and the contribution it might make to their work during their training programme.

1.6.  Trainers should ensure that practical experience of counselling under regular supervision should be part of counselling training.

1.7.  Trainers should arrange for initial, continuous, and final assessments of trainees' work and their continuing fitness for the course. Trainers should make trainees aware of this process.

1.8.  Trainers should provide opportunities for trainees to work with self individually, and in groups, so that trainees may learn to integrate professional practice and personal insights.

1.9.  Trainers should ensure that trainees are given the opportunity to discuss their experience of the course in groups, individually or both.

1.10. Trainers should encourage self-assessment and peer assessment amongst their trainees.

1.11. Trainers are to ensure that their trainees are made aware of the distinctions between counselling, managerial, and consultancy tasks and roles in training and supervision.

1.12. Trainers who become aware of a conflict between their obligation to a trainee and their obligation to an agency or organization employing them will make explicit to the trainee the nature of the loyalties involved.

1.13. Where personal differences cannot be resolved the trainer will consult with and where appropriate refer to another colleague.

1.14. Trainers should arrange for regular evaluation and assessment of their work by a professional supervisor or consultant and should ask for full and prompt information of the results.

1.15. Trainers should take account of the limitations of their competence and make appropriate arrangements when necessary.

2.  *Confidentiality*

2.1.  Confidentiality must be maintained with regard to information of a personal or sexual nature obtained by the trainer.

2.2. Trainers may not reveal confidential information concerning trainees to any other person or through any public medium except to those to whom trainers owe accountability for training work (in the case of those working within an agency or organizational setting) or on whom trainers rely for support and supervision.

2.3. Confidentiality does not preclude the disclosure of confidential information relating to trainees when relevant to the following:
   a. evaluation of the trainee by trainers or training committee.
   b. recommendations concerning trainees for professional purposes.
   c. pursuit of disciplinary action involving trainees in matters pertaining to ethical standards.
   d. selection procedures.

2.4. Information about specific trainees may only be used for publication in appropriate journals or meetings with the trainee's permission and with anonymity preserved when the trainee so specifies.

2.5. Discussion by trainers of their trainees with professional colleagues should be purposeful and not trivialising.

# BAC Code of Ethics and Practice for the Supervision of Counsellors

## A.  Introduction

A.1.  The purpose of this Code of Ethics is to establish standards for Supervisors in their supervision work with Counsellors, and to inform and protect Counsellors seeking supervision.

A.2.  Ethical standards comprise such values as integrity, competence, confidentiality and responsibility.

A.3.  This document should be seen in relation to the Code of Ethics and Practice for Counsellors.

A.4.  Members of this Association, in assenting to this Code, accept their responsibilities to counsellors and their clients, their agencies, to colleagues, and this Association.

A.5.  There are various models of supervision. The Code applies to all supervision arrangements.

The Code of Ethics has three sections:
1. The Nature of Supervision
2. Issues of Responsibility
3. Issues of Competence
The Code of Practice has two sections:
1. The Management of the Supervision Work
2. Confidentiality
The Appendix describes different models of Supervision, and comments on issues that may be relevant to particular models.

## B.  Code of ethics

### B.1.  *The nature of supervision*

1.1.  The primary purpose of supervision is to ensure that the counsellor is addressing the needs of the client.

1.2.  Supervision is a formal collaborative process. The term 'supervision' encompasses a number of functions concerned with monitoring, developing, and supporting individuals in their counselling role. (This process is sometimes known as 'non-managerial supervision' or 'consultative support'.)

1.3.  To this end supervision is concerned with:
    a) the relationship between counsellor and client, to enhance its therapeutic effectiveness.

b) monitoring and supporting the counsellor in the counselling role.

c) the relationship between the counsellor and the supervisor, in order to enable the counsellor to develop his/her professional identity through reflection on the work, in the context of this relationship, which will be both critical and supportive.

d) clarifying the relationships between counsellor, client, supervisor, and (if any) the organisation(s) involved.

e) ensuring that ethical standards are maintained throughout the counselling work.

1.4. Supervision is therefore not primarily concerned with:

a) training

b) personal counselling of the counsellor

c) line management

However, the skills associated with these activities are central to competent supervision.

1.5. The supervisory relationship must by its nature be confidential.

1.6. A counsellor should not work without regular supervision.

## B.2. *Issues of responsibility*

2.1. Given that the primary purpose of supervision is to ensure that the counsellor is addressing the needs of the client:

a) counsellors are responsible for their work with the client, and for presenting and exploring as honestly as possible that work with the supervisor.

b) Supervisors are responsible for helping counsellors reflect critically upon that work.

It is important that both parties are able to work together effectively. (See C.2.1. to C.2.4.)

2.2. Supervisors are responsible with counsellors for ensuring that they make best use of the supervision time.

2.3. Supervisors and counsellors are both responsible for setting and maintaining clear boundaries between working relationships and friendships or other relationships, and making explicit the boundaries between supervision, consultancy, therapy and training.

2.4. Supervisors and counsellors must distinguish between supervising and counselling the counsellor. They would not normally expect to mix the two. On the rare occasions when the supervisor might engage in counselling with the counsellor, a clear contract must be negotiated, and any counselling done must not be at the expense of supervision time.

2.5. Supervisors are responsible for the observation of the principles embodied in this Code of Ethics & Practice for the Supervision of Counsellors, and the Code of Ethics & Practice for Counsellors.

2.6. Supervisors must recognise the value and dignity of counsellors as people, irrespective of origin, status, sex, sexual orientation, age, belief or contribution to society.

2.7.   Supervisors are responsible for encouraging and facilitating the self-development of others, whilst also establishing clear working agreements which indicate the responsibility of counsellors for their own continued learning and self-monitoring.

2.8.   Both are responsible for regularly reviewing the effectiveness of the supervision arrangement, and considering when it is appropriate to change it.

2.9.   Supervisors are responsible for ensuring that the satisfaction of their own needs is not dependent upon the supervisory relationship, and they should not exploit this relationship.

2.10. The supervisor and counsellor should both consider their respective legal liabilities to each other, the employing organisation, if any, and the client.

## B.3.   *Issues of Competence*

3.1.   Supervisors should continually seek ways of increasing their own professional development, including, wherever possible, specific training in the development of supervision skills.

3.2.   Supervisors must monitor their supervision work and be prepared to account to their counsellors and colleagues for the work they do.

3.3.   Supervisors must monitor the limits of their competence.

3.4.   Supervisors are strongly encouraged to make arrangements for their own consultancy and support to help them evaluate their supervision work.

3.5.   Supervisors have a responsibility to monitor and maintain their own effectiveness. There may be a need to seek help and/or withdraw from the practice of supervision, whether temporarily or permanently.

3.6.   Counsellors should consider carefully the implications of choosing a supervisor who is not a practising counsellor. This applies especially to inexperienced counsellors.

## C.   Code of practice

### C.1.   *Introduction*

This Code of Practice is intended to give more specific information and guidance regarding the implementation of the principles embodied in the Code of Ethics for the Supervision of Counsellors.

### C.2.   *The Management of the Supervision Work*

In order to establish an effective supervision contract, the following points should be considered:

2.1.   Supervisors should inform counsellors as appropriate about their own training, philosophy and theoretical approach, qualifications, and the methods they use.

2.2. Supervisors should be explicit regarding practical arrangements for supervision, paying particular regard to the length of contact time, the frequency of contact and the privacy of the venue.

2.3. Fees required should be arranged in advance.

2.4. Supervisors and counsellors should make explicit the expectations and requirements they have of each other, and each party should assess the value of working with the other.

2.5. Before embarking on a supervision contract, supervisors should ascertain what, if any, therapeutic or helping relationships the counsellor has had, or is currently engaged in. This is in order to establish any effect this may have on the counsellor's counselling work.

2.6. If, in the course of supervision, it appears that counselling or therapy would be beneficial to a counsellor, the supervisor should discuss the issue and, if appropriate, make a suitable referral to a third party or agency.

2.7. Supervisors should ensure that counsellors are given regular opportunities to discuss and evaluate their experiences of supervision.

2.8. Supervisors should regularly review how the counsellor engages in self-assessment and self-evaluation of their work.

2.9. Supervisors should ensure that counsellors understand the importance of further training experiences, and encourage the counsellor's professional development in this way.

2.10. Supervisors must ensure that counsellors are made aware of the distinction between counselling, accountability to management, consultancy, support, supervision and training.

2.11. Because there is a distinction between line management and counselling supervision, where a counsellor works in an organisation or agency, the lines of accountability and responsibility need to be clearly defined, between: counsellor/client; supervisor/counsellor; organisation/client; organisation/supervisor; organisation/counsellor; supervisor/client.

2.12. Supervisors who become aware of a conflict between their obligation to a counsellor and their obligation to an employing organisation will make explicit to the counsellor the nature of the loyalties and responsibilities involved.

2.13. Where personal disagreements cannot be resolved by discussion between supervisor and counsellor, the supervisor should consult with a fellow professional and, if appropriate, offer to refer the counsellor to another supervisor.

2.14. In addition to the routine self-monitoring of their work, supervisors are strongly encouraged to arrange for regular evaluation of their work by an appropriately experienced consultant.

2.15. Supervisors should, whenever possible, seek further training experience that is relevant to their supervision work.

2.16. Supervisors should take account of the limitations of their competence, and arrange consultations or referrals when appropriate.

## C.3. *Confidentiality*

3.1   As a general principle, supervisors must maintain confidentiality with regard to information about counsellors or clients, with the exceptions cited in C.3.2, C.3.3. and C.3.4.

3.2.   Supervisors must not reveal confidential information concerning counsellors or clients to any other person or through any public medium unless:
   a) it is clearly stated in the supervision contract that this is acceptable to both parties, or
   b) when the supervisor considers it is necessary to prevent serious emotional or physical damage to the client.

   When the initial contract is being made, agreement about the people to whom a supervisor may speak must include the people on whom the supervisor relies for support, supervision or consultancy. There must also be clarity at this stage about the boundaries of confidentiality regarding people (other than the counsellor) to whom the supervisor may be accountable.

3.3.   Confidentiality does not preclude the disclosure of confidential information relating to counsellors when relevant to the following:
   a) recommendations concerning counsellors for professional purposes.
   b) pursuit of disciplinary action involving counsellors in matters pertaining to ethical standards.

3.4.   Information about specific counsellors may only be used for publication in journals or meetings with the counsellor's permission, and with anonymity preserved when the counsellor so specifies.

3.5.   Discussion by supervisors of counsellors with professional colleagues should be purposeful and not trivialising.

## D.   Appendix

## D.1. *Models of supervision*

1.1.   There are different models of supervision. This appendix outlines the particular features of some of these models.

1.2.   One-to-one: Supervisor–Counsellor:
   This involves a single supervisor providing supervision for one other counsellor, who is usually less experienced than themselves in counselling. This is still the most widely used method of supervision. Its long history means that most of the issues requiring the supervisor's and counsellor's consideration are well understood, and these are included within the Code of Practice above.

1.3.   One-to-one: Co-supervision:
   This involves two participants providing supervision for each other by alternating the roles of supervisor and counsellor. Typically, the time available for a supervision session is divided equally between them.

1.4. Group supervision with identified supervisor(s):
There are a range of ways of providing this form of supervision. At one end of the spectrum the supervisor, acting as the leader, will take responsibility for apportioning the time between the counsellors, and then concentrating on the work of individuals in turn. At the other end of the range, the counsellors will allocate supervision time between themselves, using the supervisor as a technical resource. There are many different ways of working between these two alternatives.

1.5. Peer group supervision:
This takes place when three or more counsellors share the responsibility for providing each others' supervision within a group context. Typically, they will consider themselves to be of broadly equal status, training and/or experience.

1.6. Eclectic methods of supervision:
Some counsellors use combinations of the above models for their supervision.

## D.2. *Points requiring additional consideration*

2.1. Certain models require the consideration of some of the points listed below, that are additional to the contents of the Code of Practice.

| Types of Supervision (See below D.2): | Points for Consideration |||||||| 
|---|---|---|---|---|---|---|---|---|
| | 2 | 3 | 4 | 5 | 6 | 7 | 8 | 9 |
| D1.2. One-to-one: Supervisor–Counsellor | X | | | | | | | |
| D1.3. One-to-one: Co-supervision | X | X | X | X | | | | |
| D1.4. Group supervision with identified supervisors | | X | X | X | X | X | | |
| D1.5. Peer group supervision | X | X | X | X | – | X | X | X |
| D1.6. Eclectic model | All revelant points. | | | | | | | |

2.2. All the points contained elsewhere within the Code of Practice should be considered.

2.3. Sufficient time must be allocated to each counsellor to ensure adequate supervision of the counselling work.

2.4. This method is unlikely to be suitable for newly trained or inexperienced counsellors, because of the importance of supervisors being experienced in counselling.

2.5. Care needs to be taken to develop an atmosphere conducive to sharing, questioning and challenging each others' practice in a constructive way.

2.6. As well as having a background in counselling work, supervisors should have appropriate groupwork experience in order to facilitate this kind of group.

2.7.  All the participants should have sufficient groupwork experience to be able to engage the group process in ways in which facilitate effective supervision.

2.8.  Explicit consideration should be given to deciding who is responsible for providing the supervision, and how the task of supervision will be carried out.

2.9.  It is desirable that these groups are visited from time to time by a consultant to observe the group process and monitor the quality of the supervision.